The Media Training Bible

101 THINGS YOU ABSOLUTELY, POSITIVELY NEED TO KNOW BEFORE YOUR NEXT INTERVIEW

Brad Phillips

D1430320

SpeakGood Press
1050 17th Street NW, Suite 600
Washington, DC 20036

ISBN-10: 0988322005

EAN-13: 9780988322004

Library of Congress Control Number: 2012917377
SpeakGood Press, Washington, DC

Praise for The Media Training Bible

"*The Media Training Bible* is a must read for learning best practices for creating, delivering, and staying on message with the media—a reference you'll want on your top shelf."

Wayne Bloom, CEO, Commonwealth Financial Network

"If more politicians read *The Media Training Bible*, there would be many fewer embarrassing stories about them featured on Political Wire."

Taegan Goddard, Founder and Publisher, Political Wire
(www.politicalwire.com)

"In a chaotic media landscape, Brad Phillips offers a thorough and engaging guide to getting your message out authentically and effectively. Take Brad's advice to heart. The little things do matter. I've witnessed a man's ill-chosen words on national television implode his career, and a woman who handled a difficult interview so well she transcended the controversy swirling around her. Brad can help you avoid the former and execute the latter."

Richard Harris, Former Director of Afternoon Programming, National Public Radio and Former Senior Producer, ABC News *Nightline*

"Through a perfect mix of lessons, case studies, and exercises, Brad Phillips unlocks the secrets of becoming an effective spokesperson. I refer to *The Media Training Bible* before every interview—and you will too."

Tod Ibrahim, Executive Director, The American Society of Nephrology

"Everyone who speaks to the media—and anyone who might— should read *The Media Training Bible* before even thinking about doing another interview. Executives and other professionals will want to keep this invaluable resource within reaching distance for many years to come."

Russ Mittermeier, President, Conservation International

"*The Media Training Bible* is the most comprehensive and well-reasoned resource on this topic I have ever read. Well-organized and thorough, it contains everything necessary to prepare readers for contact with the media, regardless of whether they are a novice or a seasoned veteran. Brad Phillips leverages his unique background as an ex-member of the media and an active media trainer and commentator to create a powerful resource that can be used again and again. Public relations professionals—and the executives they serve— shouldn't be out there without it."

Linda Carlisle, Corporate Communications Manager, Elkay Manufacturing Company

"*The Media Training Bible* goes far beyond the standard media training guides and is must-reading for anyone who would be the least bit frightened by an unexpected knock on the door from the local TV news crew. Brad Phillips' 101 lessons will arm you with everything you need to know to be interviewed by even the toughest bulldog reporter and not only survive, but thrive, in the spotlight. More than three dozen case studies show you how to avoid costly mistakes made by celebrities, politicians and others who didn't understand the confusing rules of the media game. (The media know the rules, but they don't want YOU to know.) Don't pitch stories and don't accept requests for media interviews until you read this book."

Joan Stewart, Publisher, The Publicity Hound (www.publicityhound.com)

"Brad Phillips' book will become *THE* Media Training Bible for CEOs, leaders, and spokespersons who want to be a winner with the media. Phillips shares what reporters need, how to craft your message, and how to deliver it simply and effectively in every medium. It's loaded with practical, tactical and proven advice from a true media training pro. After 30 years of PR consulting and media training myself, I've never seen the topic so well organized and practically delivered."

Jeff Domansky, The PR Coach (www.theprcoach.com)

"Brad Phillips has produced an excellent resource with *The Media Training Bible*. It does in fact live up to its promise with over 100 lessons in what to do, say, and think (or not to do, say or think) before ever embarking on the often treacherous journey into 'MediaLand.' The book is very comprehensive, a compelling read, and very practical. I highly recommend it—a must for anyone contemplating a media spokesperson role.

Jane Jordan-Meier, Crisis Coach and Author, *The Four Stages of Highly Effective Crisis Management: How to Manage the Media in the Digital Age*

"The key to success with media interviews is preparation. *The Media Training Bible* is one of the most insightful and easy-to-use resources for communications professionals and business executives to prepare for any type of interview."

Dave Groobert, U.S. General Manager, Environics Communications

"The advice in *The Media Training Bible* is both timely and timeless, filled with hands-on guidance that can be applied immediately."

Michael Sebastian, Managing Editor, Ragan's PR Daily (www.prdaily.com)

Table of Contents

Foreword by Michael Sebastian, Managing Editor, PR Daily

We live in the age of the headline.

To grab a person's attention, news organizations have roughly the time it takes a person to read a headline before their eyes are pulled somewhere else. With such frayed attention spans, today's news consumer increasingly wants their information packaged and sold to them in seven-second sound bites and 140-character tweets.

Even in today's fast-paced media culture, there are ways to present a cohesive message. But it requires training and practice, even for straightforward interviews with a reporter you know well. You want to answer the reporter's question honestly while conveying your message, and do all of it without sounding canned or robotic. It's a tricky business.

Brad Phillips understands this, because he is a former journalist, having served under ABC News's Ted Koppel and CNN's Wolf Blitzer. In *The Media Training Bible*, he'll share what he learned both inside the newsroom and in the media training studio room. You will find tips that will make you a more effective spokesperson, rules of the road for working with journalists, and important advice on body language and attire. You'll learn how to create a winning message that appeals to journalists *and* the public. You'll also find guidance on how to prepare for and manage a PR crisis, an essential component of any spokesperson's job—especially in the age of the headline.

Often, an organization will stumble into a PR crisis because the person speaking on its behalf is not prepared to talk to the media. Sometimes, even well-prepared speakers can commit a blunder by briefly straying from their message. This is what the media likes to call a "gaffe," and it will haunt spokespersons and CEOs.

Take, for instance, the Deepwater Horizon disaster. In April 2010, an explosion on the Deepwater Horizon oil rig in the Gulf of Mexico killed 11 workers aboard and unleashed an oil spill that lasted for three months. To date, it is the largest accidental marine petroleum spill in the history of the oil industry.

The incident also stands as one of the worst PR disasters in modern history. BP, the company that owned the well from which the leak sprung, committed a series of blunders that made it look incompetent, reckless, and tone deaf. Chief among them was this jaw-dropper from then-CEO Tony Hayward:

> "I'm sorry. We're sorry for the massive disruption it's caused their lives. There's no one who wants this over more than I do. *I'd like my life back* [italics mine]."

Hayward was trying to apologize. Instead of the reporters echoing his mea culpa, they repeated those five words—"I'd like my life back"—in endless rotation. It's a juicy sound bite for TV, and the ideal length for a tweet.

Organizations and public figures must prepare for media scrutiny. This preparation isn't about spin or subterfuge but instead media training. It's about knowing *who* will speak to the media, *what* they will say, and *how* often they will say it. An ethical, media-trained spokesperson should serve as a resource for journalists, not as a roadblock. Journalists will respect a spokesperson who is informed, upfront, and honest.

Media spokespersons and public relations professionals can pull *The Media Training Bible* from the shelf to prepare for media interviews and refer to it when drafting their crisis communications plans. The advice is both timely and timeless, filled with hands-on guidance that can be applied immediately. I am confident that *The Media Training Bible* will prove a useful resource for organizations of any size, public or private, nonprofit or for profit.

Preface:
The State of the Media Today

Are the traditional media—newspapers, radio stations, and television networks—breathing their last breaths, barely clinging to life as the "new" media steal their audiences?

It would be easy to make that case. Hundreds of once-popular U.S. newspapers have either collapsed or shifted to an online-only platform over the past 20-some years. Others have watched their audiences evaporate. Since 1990, newspapers including the *Los Angeles Times, New York Daily News, San Francisco Chronicle, Chicago Sun-Times,* and the *Boston Globe* have seen their circulations slashed by at least half—and they're far from alone.

The decline in viewership for the network evening newscasts is just as stark. In 1990, 41 million viewers tuned in to ABC, CBS, or NBC each night to watch the evening news. Two decades later, just 22 million did. Why rush home by 6:30 p.m. to watch a news program when you can now watch one at 7 p.m. instead? Or 8 p.m.? Or anytime, online and on demand?

Whereas we once depended upon Tom Brokaw to deliver the news of the day, we now reach into our pockets, grab our smartphones, and select the news for ourselves. We read, listen to, or watch the news stories we want from the sources we choose—around the clock, at our convenience—on blogs, DVRs, iPads, podcasts, Twitter feeds, and countless other devices.

According to some media observers, even the biggest news organizations—*The New York Times, The Washington Post, Time* magazine—could soon be gone, at least in the forms they currently exist.

Not so fast. It's true that the traditional media are hurting, and the shift away from traditional media is indeed profound. In 2011, for example,

Americans got more of their news online than from newspapers for the first time ever.

But traditional media continue to wield enormous influence over our national debate and will do so for decades to come. Newspapers, radio stations, and television news programs still reach more than 100 million Americans each day through their traditional forms—and tens of millions more through their online outlets. Readers give stories from traditional news outlets additional reach by sharing them with their social networks, expanding the audience of local news organizations to people in other cities, states, and nations.

To be sure, the impact of social media on news has revolutionized the entire media landscape. No longer is news the exclusive province of a paternal newsman. Blogs often break news first (sometimes due to lower standards for confirming information), citizen journalists occasionally provide the first bloody pictures of national revolution, and public figures frequently make newsworthy pronouncements using their own social media accounts.

Still, it's an overstatement to claim the traditional media are dying while their younger brethren are taking over. A more accurate description would account for the symbiosis between the two; the old media feed off of the new media and vice versa. Bloggers analyze news first reported by "stodgier" newspapers. Radio newscasters report on a controversial remark someone made on Twitter. Facebook users share a link to a story they originally saw on a cable news program. Network newscasts show video that first went "viral" on YouTube.

Today's traditional and new media live side by side, strongly influencing the tone, pace, and content of the other. And that means that the lines separating the two aren't always clear.

Media training requires that spokespersons are equipped for traditional *and* new media. The skill sets for both are similar but not identical. This book will prepare you for today's media culture, in which a tweet can become newsworthy and a news interview can become tweet-worthy.

"Journalists are accused of being lapdogs when they don't ask the hard questions, but then accused of being rude when they do. Good thing we have tough hides."

Gwen Ifill, Journalist

Introduction

Every day, I receive phone calls from potential new clients seeking media training.

When I ask what concerns prompted their calls, they almost always say the same things: "We're not good at getting our messages across," or, "I tend to say too much, and I'm afraid the audience isn't getting my point," or, "I'm terrified of going on television, but it's my responsibility as the executive director to do so."

Toward the end of the conversation, many callers ask—often skeptically—whether we can help. They wonder whether a day of media training can truly make them feel more confident and in control during an interview.

It can.

I often ask the callers to rate their media skills on a scale of 1 to 10. If they score themselves a 5, I tell them they can become a 7 in just one day of training. Our clients regularly leap a couple of notches in just a few hours simply by learning how to identify and focus on the areas that most impede their effectiveness. By removing their own roadblocks, budding spokespersons experience noticeable, often dramatic, and occasionally shocking growth.

My goal for this book is to help you achieve the same growth without me being there in person (and for thousands of dollars less than we charge our private clients). You really can go from a 5 to a 7—or whatever your equivalent—simply by reading this book. And I wouldn't be surprised if you jumped more than two notches, but I'd rather underpromise and over-deliver.

Almost everyone we work with has the capacity to improve, no matter how great their challenges. It's true that some people are born with the tremendous gift of being captivating communicators, but that's not the case for most people you see on television. They blew an interview or two early on and suffered a few media missteps along the way. But they stuck with it, nurtured their communications skills, adjusted their approaches, and improved over time.

You can too.

Great spokespersons know that it doesn't matter if you stumble over a few words once in a while or lose your train of thought on occasion. You don't have to be perfect—in fact, the public often regards "perfect" spokespersons as slick and inauthentic. If you're a perfectionist, I'm going to ask you to try your hardest to abandon your perfectionism—it will only get in your way and inhibit your most effective self from stepping forward.

You may be pleasantly surprised to learn that you already share some traits with the world's most gifted spokespersons. Most of the greats, regardless of personal style, ideology, or cause, have the following six traits in common:

First, they're authentic. The audience may not agree with their perspectives, but viewers can tell that the spokespersons genuinely believe in their own messages.

Second, they're natural. The best spokespersons are the ones the public perceives as being the same person on camera as off, the same in a television studio as in their living room. They're the spokespersons who bring the same passion to their interviews that they express privately when discussing similar topics with their friends.

Third, they're flexible. They know that breaking news, technical issues, or a shifting storyline can change the nature of their interview with little notice. They know that rolling with the changes, maintaining their composure, and displaying a touch of humor—where appropriate—will enhance the audience's impression of them.

Fourth, they speak to their audience. They know that their primary function during an interview isn't to impress their bosses or peers, but to forge a direct connection with each person reading or hearing their words.

Fifth, they self-edit. Great media spokespersons know that their job is to reduce information to its most essential parts, never to "dumb down" but always to simplify. They know not to try to say *everything*, since doing so muddles their message and confuses their audience.

Sixth, they're compelling. They know how to express their points in an engaging manner that helps their audience remember them. They know how to use stories, statistics, and sound bites to make their messages stand out, and are adept at coining phrases that stick in the minds of every audience member.

Here's the bottom line: if you're capable of energetically delivering a credible and memorable message that you genuinely believe in, the audience is likely to perceive you favorably.

Possessing those six traits, while critically important, won't guarantee media success. You've probably noticed that even the most experienced spokespersons occasionally say the wrong thing or respond with the wrong tone. Almost every day brings another high-profile example of a public figure committing a humiliating media mistake, whether it's a politician whose offhanded remark costs him an election, a CEO whose thoughtless comment causes her company's stock price to plummet, or a nonprofit executive whose answer makes clear he doesn't truly "get" the scandal that's engulfed his organization.

This book will teach you how to avoid committing the types of media mistakes that lead to humiliating headlines, embarrassing television stories, and disastrous YouTube video clips.

As you'll see in the pages that follow, most media mistakes are preventable. Too often, I see spokespersons who offer tentative replies instead of powerful messages, appear defensive instead of self-assured, deliver monotone responses instead of infusing their quotes with the passion they genuinely feel, and commit the deadly "seven-second stray" that takes them far away from their intended message.

Even when they do everything perfectly, they worry about their intended message making it past the media middleman. Our clients frequently—and quite understandably—express dismay that the era of unbiased journalism (to the degree it ever existed) is in decline, only to be replaced by a form of journalism that prioritizes opinion and sensationalism over facts and information. It's little surprise that many spokespersons have encountered a dishonest reporter, dealt with a biased news organization, or suffered from an incorrect story that spread across Twitter in the blink of an eye—or the click of a mouse. As a result, they turn a jaundiced eye toward the media as a whole.

Many of their objections about the media are accurate. But I don't usually linger on that point for long. That's because while none of us has the power to change the way the media operate, we *do* have the power to effectively work within the confines of today's flawed media culture to reach our audiences and achieve our goals.

Despite what you may have heard (or personally experienced), most reporters aren't out to get you. More often than not, they just want reliable information from a spokesperson who can deliver a media-friendly quote. Sure, you may occasionally face aggressive reporters— and this book will prepare you for them— but you'll more commonly face ones who want little more than to file accurate and engaging stories.

So it's well worth your effort to build constructive relationships with the press. Positive media stories can inspire legions of people to buy your products, support your ideas, and vote for your preferred candidate. They can help you build your business, grow your name recognition, and enhance your reputation.

I've worked in and around media for close to two decades. I remain absolutely convinced of the tremendous opportunities that news stories can deliver for you and your brand.

ABOUT THIS BOOK

My objective in writing this book was simple: I wanted to provide readers with the most comprehensive book on media training ever written.

In the pages that follow, you will find 101 lessons, 36 real-life case studies, a web address to access more than a dozen videos, and numerous exercises.

The case studies will bring to life the media training techniques you'll soon learn. Some are entertaining and others are horrifying, but all are instructive.

Although I've done my best to explain the case studies featured in this book, my descriptions are no match for seeing the videos for yourself. You'll notice a (V) mark next to the titles of selected case studies. That symbol means you can view the video at www.MrMediaTraining. com/Book/Videos.

You will also find several exercises throughout the book. These exercises are your opportunities to make this book relevant to your own work, so I hope you'll spend some time working through them. When you finish, you will have three winning media messages supported by compelling stories, statistics, and sound bites. You will also learn the best way to prepare for a media interview, an effective method for conducting crisis drills, and a technique to help you eliminate the "uhhhs" and "ummms" that plague speakers.

This book is organized as 101 two-page lessons divided into eight sections:

> In **Section One** you will learn eight crucial ground rules for working with reporters.
>
> **Section Two** teaches you how to create compelling media messages and develop the "message supports" that make them even more memorable.

In **Section Three** you will learn how to master the art of the interview.

Section Four offers techniques that will help you answer even the toughest questions with (relative) ease.

Section Five helps you understand what your body language communicates and what your attire says about you.

In **Section Six** you will learn more about the different media formats and how to navigate each of them with ease.

Section Seven highlights the 10 truths of a crisis and arms you with tools to counteract negative press.

Section Eight guides you through the final steps you should take when preparing for media interviews.

Finally, the **Conclusion** provides you with resources for additional learning and offers you guidance for selecting a media trainer should you decide to pursue in-person training for yourself or your colleagues.

The advice contained in this book has been successfully field-tested by thousands of our trainees over the past decade. I, along with the other professional media trainers who work for my firm, have watched the techniques described in this book work for almost all of the media interviews our clients have delivered. Although no book can account for every possible scenario, we're confident that these techniques will help guide you through the majority of them.

I encourage you to read the entire book rather than skipping ahead to a single section. The techniques in this book build upon one another, and almost every skill influences the next. For example, you might be interested primarily in learning about proper body language. But you may be surprised to learn that almost everyone *automatically* has better body language once they become more comfortable with their message. Your words and performance work in alignment with one another, and it is difficult to succeed at one without succeeding at both.

One final note: You will learn hundreds of pointers throughout this book. Don't worry about mastering all of them right away. A brief self-analysis toward the end of the book will help you narrow everything you've learned down to the three things you need to focus on most. Only when you become more comfortable with those three things should you add a fourth, then a fifth, and so on.

By purchasing this book, you've expressed your commitment to gaining the skills and confidence you need to excel in every media interview you deliver. I'm delighted you've placed your trust in me.

Let's get started!

Eight Ground Rules
For Working With The Media

*"It is always a risk to speak to the press:
they are likely to report what you say."*

Hubert Humphrey, U.S. Vice President (1965—1969)

1 THE RULE OF THIRDS

The very first question to ask yourself when a reporter requests an interview with you is this: "Should I agree to the interview?"

Most of the time, the answer is "yes." But not always. You might consider turning down an interview in these scenarios:

- The topic isn't relevant to your work.

- The topic isn't company specific (for example, if a journalist is writing about how the recession is hurting local businesses, you might not want your brand to be associated with the idea of a bad economy).

- You would gain absolutely nothing by doing the interview (and even then, it's occasionally worth doing).

But if the story is about your company *and* will be written with or without your participation, you should probably agree to the interview. Here's why: There are three voices in many news stories—yours, your opponent's, and the reporter's. If you refuse the interview, "The Rule of Thirds" states that you'll likely go 0-for-3 in the story.

1/3 YOUR VOICE	1/3 OPPONENT'S VOICE	1/3 REPORTER'S VOICE

That's because your opponent will almost surely be critical of you in their one-third of the story, and reporters may hold your refusal to comment against you by slanting the tone of *their* one-third in favor of your opponent. That may not be fair, but reporters tend to provide more sympathetic coverage to sources who talk to them. They might even give your opponents additional airtime since you didn't claim any of it for yourself.

Speaking to the reporter doesn't guarantee you a positive story. But it's still usually worth agreeing to the interview since going 1-for-3 is a whole lot better than not scoring at all. Plus, your participation in the story makes clear to the public that you're not in "duck and cover" mode.

It's worth noting that some news stories don't include an "opponent's" voice. But journalists are inclined to include one wherever possible, since conflict makes for more dramatic copy. In the context of a news story, your opponent may be a business that sells a competitive product, a local citizens group that opposes your nonprofit's work, a policy expert who has reached a contrary conclusion from you, or a political candidate who is vying for the same statehouse seat.

The Rule of Thirds has one additional part: don't make your opponents' case. That might sound obvious, but it's a challenge for people who feel uncomfortable presenting their side of an argument without acknowledging that the other side has merits as well.

For example, in a typical conversation, you might say:

> *"Sure, our competitor's product has some nice bells and whistles, but we believe our product is overwhelmingly superior."*

But a reporter might choose to quote only a small portion of your response:

> *"Our competitor's product has some nice bells and whistles."*

Let your competitors make the case for themselves in their own one-third. Your job is to use your one-third to fully advance your own cause, not to provide "balance." It's a safe bet that your opponent won't provide balance for you in return.

2 MEETING A REPORTER'S DEADLINE ISN'T ENOUGH

Many media relations experts advise that you should always return phone calls from reporters *by* their deadlines.

That's terrible advice—or at least terribly *incomplete* advice.

Let's say Dan, a local newspaper reporter, calls you at 9 a.m. He tells you he's working on a story related to your company's product for tomorrow's paper and needs a quote from you by 4 p.m. today.

If you wait until 3:50 p.m. to return his call, you officially met his deadline, right? Well, not really. By the time you return Dan's call, he's probably already completed 95 percent of his story. That means he'll just insert your quote somewhere into his piece to make sure your viewpoint is represented.

But by waiting that long, you did little to help shape his story angle, increase his understanding of your issues, or refer him to your allies (and less vehement opponents) for their comments. As a result, the story will be comprised mostly of the reporter's perspective and those of everyone else he's spoken to, not yours. Your quote won't have much impact.

Instead, ask Dan for more details about what he'd like to discuss and tell him you'll return his call by 10 a.m. Dan may tell you he's on deadline to pressure you into speaking immediately. Don't. This isn't an improv class. Use that hour to prepare for the interview, and call him back as soon as you're ready.

Calling him back by 10 a.m. means you've probably reached him before he's written the article's first word, giving you a terrific opportunity to help shape his perspective and influence his final story. It also means he won't feel as compelled to find alternate sources, increasing your presence in the article.

You can also invite Dan to call you later in the day to verify any facts or discuss anything he learned after speaking with other sources, including your opponents. Many reporters will take you up on your offer, giving you two solid bites at the interviewing apple instead of just one measly nibble.

It's important to note that although some reporters use deadlines as a pressure tactic to get you to speak immediately, some reporters really *are* on deadline. That's especially true for reporters pursuing a breaking news story, writing for the web, or contacting you shortly before they go to air or put the issue "to bed."

If you're faced with a decision of talking to an on-deadline reporter immediately or being left out of the story, decide which of the two comes with the greater risk. As lesson one explained, it's generally better to speak if the story is going to be about you anyway. But in some cases, it might be more prudent to turn down the interview, request more time, or "comment without commenting" (more on that in lesson four) if you haven't given the topic much thought and could create a larger problem by doing the interview and saying the wrong thing.

Either way, here's the correct advice for most interactions: return a reporter's call as quickly as possible, well *before* the deadline.

NEWS DEADLINES: A GENERAL GUIDE

- Daily newspapers: Late afternoon
- Weekly newspapers or magazines: Depends on day of release; most commonly Wednesday—Friday
- Monthly magazines: Two or three months before issue date
- Radio and television: One or two hours before broadcast
- Internet: Rolling deadlines, sometimes 24 hours a day

3 WHY "NO COMMENT" IS A NO-NO

Imagine you were in the room when one tobacco executive invoked his Fifth Amendment protection against self-incrimination 97 times *in a single deposition.* If you're like most people, your first reaction would have been to think "Guilty!"

There is no phrase more damning in a spokesperson's lexicon than "no comment." Fairly or not, the public regards a person who utters those words the same way they view a person who shouts "I did it!" into a megaphone in a crowded park. (If anything, the person in the park is probably regarded more favorably, since the public often awards bonus points for honesty.)

> *There is no phrase more damning in a spokesperson's lexicon than "no comment."*

Reporters also view "no comment" with suspicion and may frame their stories in a manner that makes the person who said it look guilty.

A newspaper reporter might write, "CEO Bill Truman refused to comment when asked whether these charges were true." A television correspondent might show video of the CEO walking hurriedly away from his microphone.

The exact words "no comment" aren't the only ones that do damage. *Anything* that conveys the same sentiment has the same negative effect.

That doesn't mean you have to tell a reporter everything you know. There are often legitimate reasons for withholding information, and you'll learn how to avoid commenting on tough topics without saying "no comment" in the next lesson.

CASE STUDY: MARK MCGWIRE
TESTIFIES BEFORE CONGRESS (V)

Baseball slugger Mark McGwire broke the all-time single season home run record in 1998, but his achievement was tainted by rumors regarding his use of performance-enhancing drugs.

In 2005, Congress subpoenaed McGwire to testify at a hearing about steroids. When asked whether he had taken steroids, McGwire replied, "I'm not here to talk about the past," a phrase he repeated nine times in just a few minutes.

Although he didn't confess, it didn't matter. The public took his evasion to mean the same as "I took steroids" and convicted him of being a cheat. McGwire became a pariah, stripped of his hero's status and banished from the game he loved.

In 2010, he finally admitted what everybody already knew—that he had taken steroids. Although his admission paved the way just enough for him to re-enter professional baseball as a coach, his reputation remains severely tarnished.

The surest sign of McGwire's damaged standing? Voters to the National Baseball Hall of Fame have consistently rejected his inclusion to the Hall by an overwhelming margin.

4 COMMENT WITHOUT COMMENTING

Just because you shouldn't use the phrase "no comment" doesn't mean you have to reveal everything you know to every reporter who asks. There are many times when you truly cannot or should not answer a reporter's question.

These seven cases illustrate times you might withhold comment:

1. **Confidential Employee or Patient Records:** A reporter asks you for an employee file or information contained in a patient's private health record.

2. **Impending Layoffs:** The press gets wind of upcoming layoffs a few days before employees are notified, but you don't want employees to learn their fate through the media.

3. **Labor Action:** Your employees are about to go on strike (or are on strike), but you made an agreement with the union that neither side would negotiate in public.

4. **Sensitive Negotiations or Deals:** You are negotiating a sensitive deal that could be undermined by speaking to the press.

5. **Competitive Information:** You work for a privately held company and a reporter wants financial or technical information that could give a competitor an edge.

6. **Lawsuits:** You receive guidance from your attorney not to comment on an ongoing legal action, especially when the risks of communicating outweigh the risks of *not* communicating (more on this in lesson 88).

7. **Death or Injury:** An employee has been killed or seriously injured, and you would like to notify the family before confirming the news to the media.

In all seven of those examples, your strategy should be to "comment without commenting," or to offer a response that explains *why* you cannot answer the question. For example, if a journalist asks about an ongoing labor action, you might say:

> *"We promised the union that we wouldn't negotiate through the media, and we intend to honor that commitment. I will say that we want our employees to be compensated fairly. We hope to reach a deal soon that both protects our business and pays our employees the competitive salary they deserve."*

If you represent a privately held company and are asked how much profit a new product generated last year, you might say:

> *"We don't release financial information on specific products, because doing so could give our competitors an unfair advantage. What I can tell you is that the product was significantly more profitable than we anticipated."*

CASE STUDY: PRESIDENT OBAMA ON CNN

In June 2010, President Obama appeared on CNN's *Larry King Live* to discuss immigration reform. He deflected one question by commenting without commenting:

> *Mr. King: "You met with the Arizona governor today. Will the administration bring a legal challenge to this law?"*
>
> *President Obama: "I'm not going to comment on that, Larry, because that's really the job of the Justice Department, and I made a commitment early on that I wouldn't be putting my thumb on the scales [of justice] when these kinds of decisions are made."*

Although the president came perilously close to uttering the words "no comment," he nicely transitioned to his explanation for why he couldn't answer the question.

5 WHY IT'S RISKY TO GO "OFF THE RECORD"

Journalists don't really understand the phrase "off the record"— or, more precisely, they can't agree on what it means. If you speak to 10 different journalists, you'll probably hear 10 different definitions.

In fact, one survey of five reporters from separate sections of *The Washington Post* found that each of the journalists defined "off the record" differently. Some thought it meant they couldn't *ever* use information they learned; others thought the information was fair game as long as they didn't identify their source. One of the reporters even admitted, "I have no idea what 'off the record' means."

If journalists themselves can't agree on the definition of "off the record," you shouldn't rely on the term to forge agreements with reporters. It's a meaningless expression. Banish it from your lexicon.

You probably shouldn't be speaking off the record anyway. Most reporters keep their word, but some break their agreements. As former CNN correspondent Jamie McIntyre once quipped, "Just to be clear and so there is no misunderstanding, when we say off the record, we mean not for reporting in any form—unless it's *really, really* good." It's worth noting that even the most well-intentioned reporters can get overruled by their editors.

Another hazard of going off the record is that courts don't recognize agreements between a reporter and a source as a sacred trust. Judges can force journalists to disclose their sources under threat of imprisonment—and when faced with that unappetizing option, many journalists squeal. That means the reporter may still identify you by name as the source regardless of any agreement you might have had in place.

Unless you're fully prepared to take all of these risks, don't go off the record.

It's true that providing a reporter with background information may occasionally help your cause, but doing so can come with significant risks. The next lesson will offer you a few strategies to help minimize those hazards if you decide to share background information with reporters.

DEFINITIONS:
OFF THE RECORD AND OTHER JOURNALISM TERMS

Below are the most commonly accepted definitions of a few key terms, but be careful—the journalist you speak to may interpret these phrases differently.

OFF THE RECORD: Strictly speaking, off the record means that the information you share with a reporter cannot be used in a news story in any way and can only serve to help the journalist develop a more complete understanding of the facts. But beware: Some reporters may use the information if they can get a different source to confirm it.

ON BACKGROUND: The information provided by a source can be used, but the source cannot be named or quoted.

NOT FOR ATTRIBUTION: The information provided by a source may be used and the spokesperson may be quoted, but not by name. Instead, the quote will be attributed to a veiled source, such as a "senior White House official" or a "company director." Sources can (and should) negotiate with the reporter the manner in which they are described.

ON THE RECORD: Unless you specify otherwise and gain the prior agreement of the reporter, assume that everything you say is on the record. Almost all of your interviews should fall into this category.

6   IF YOU GO OFF THE RECORD ANYWAY

Experienced spokespersons occasionally opt to speak off the record or on background despite the risks of doing so.

For example, say you represent one of ten advocacy groups that are working with a politician on a specific bill. You're afraid that the politician is backing away from his promise to support the bill, but you can't criticize him publicly without risking your relationship with him. Speaking to a reporter on background might result in a media story that puts public pressure on the politician *without* compromising your personal relationship (it might be tough for him to know which of the 10 groups spoke to the press).

You might consider going on background or off the record in the following circumstances:

- You are a whistleblower who feels a moral obligation to expose corruption within a government agency.

- You are talking about a competitor and have information about a serious safety defect in your rival's product.

- You are aware that a political opponent cheated on a tax return but want to avoid the appearance of mudslinging.

Before speaking off the record or on background, you should:

1. Consult with a communications professional, either in your own company or from an outside firm.

2. Consider your relationship with the reporter. Journalists who have treated you fairly for years are generally safer bets than reporters you've never worked with before.

3. Ask reporters to tell you what off the record or on background means to them.

4. Make any agreements with reporters *before* you say something you want kept off the record. You can't give an interesting tidbit and declare it off-limits afterward.

Still, my warning bears repeating one final time: If you can't afford the risk of being named in the story, remain on the record and say only what you'd be comfortable seeing in print.

CASE STUDY: A TOP MILITARY OFFICIAL GOES OFF THE RECORD

General Stanley McChrystal, the commander of U.S. forces in Afghanistan, granted *Rolling Stone* reporter Michael Hastings unprecedented access to him and his senior staff in 2010.

For four weeks, Hastings followed the four-star general and his staff from Paris to Berlin to Afghanistan. As the military brass got increasingly comfortable with Hastings' presence, they made provocative statements about Washington's top leadership, used profane language, and got drunk with him.

The published article was a disaster for McChrystal. The story reported his unfavorable views of his bosses—including President Obama and Vice President Biden—and he was immediately summoned to Washington.

Gen. McChrystal's senior staff members protested, claiming Mr. Hastings had broken an off-the-record agreement to keep the most controversial comments out of print. One military official told *The Washington Post* that the command's review of events "...found 'no evidence to suggest' that any of the 'salacious political quotes' in the article were made in situations in which ground rules permitted Hastings to use the material in his story."

Their complaints didn't matter. Just two days after the article's publication, McChrystal was forced to resign, his prestigious 34-year military career felled by an off-the-record interview.

7 WHY THERE'S NO SUCH THING AS AN "OFFICIAL" INTERVIEW

Imagine you have a television interview scheduled with a reporter. The handsome TV news personality arrives at your office, the crew sets up the cameras and lights, and the interview begins.

Fifteen minutes fly by in what seem like seconds, and before you know it, the interview is over. You feel good. Even though the reporter asked a few tricky questions, you were prepared and handled them well.

As the crew packs up, you make some polite small talk with the reporter. He casually asks you about one of your competitors, and you make a mildly negative comment about their work. When the piece airs, you're shocked to find that the reporter introduces the story by quoting your offhand, off-camera remark about your competitor.

You may feel betrayed, but the reporter didn't do anything wrong. The interview didn't officially "begin" when the cameraman pressed the record button or "end" when he turned it off. Anything you say before, during, or after the "official" interview—including any telephone or email exchanges—can be quoted in a news story.

> *Anything you say before, during, or after the "official" interview—including any telephone or email exchanges—can be quoted in a news story.*

That doesn't mean you should avoid talking to reporters in the downtime before and after the "official" interview. But use that time to restate your most important messages—not verbatim, but by advancing the main themes you want them to remember.

CASE STUDY: CARLY FIORINA'S HAIRY SITUATION (V)

In June 2010, former Hewlett-Packard CEO Carly Fiorina won her primary bid to become California's Republican candidate for the U.S. Senate.

The morning after her win, Ms. Fiorina sat in a television studio awaiting a post-victory interview with a local Sacramento news program. Seconds before the interview began, Ms. Fiorina turned to an aide and made a nasty comment about her Democratic opponent, Senator Barbara Boxer.

She scoffed, "[A friend] saw Barbara Boxer briefly on television this morning and said what everyone says—'God, what is that hair? Sooo yesterday.'"

Ms. Fiorina stopped herself when she realized she was being recorded. But it was too late. CNN posted the raw tape on its website, fueling an unfortunate story line about Fiorina's "catty" remarks. The next day's headlines focused more on her "hair" comments than on her victory, creating a public relations nightmare for her campaign.

Ms. Fiorina never fully recovered. In a political year that favored the Republican Party, she lost to Boxer by double digits.

8 KNOW YOUR RIGHTS

Many high-powered executives, accustomed to directing their subordinates, instruct reporters to send them a draft of their articles before publication. Most reporters will not only reject that request but also resent that the executive treated them like an employee requiring approval.

Journalists have no obligation to share their final stories with you, so don't ask them to. But you have other rights that can help tilt the balance of power in your direction.

OFFER TO FACT-CHECK

Offering to "fact-check" a story is different than requesting to see a story prior to publication. Whereas asking a reporter to see a story in advance suggests a controlling executive, offering to check an article's key facts—in particular, complicated details or technical points—is usually regarded as helpful.

If reporters take you up on your offer, they might email you the entire story or have an editor call you to review a single statistic. You should focus your feedback primarily on the *facts* of the story, but you're welcome to challenge the reporter's subjective interpretations of the facts (although that might make them less inclined to ask you to fact check in the future). You may not agree with their conclusions, but they are entitled to draw them.

REQUEST QUESTIONS IN ADVANCE (SOMETIMES)

Most reporters working for major news organizations will not share their specific questions with you prior to an interview (they are usually willing to share the general premises of their stories). These "hard news" reporters regard their questions as confidential until the moment they're asked and fear that sharing them with you will tilt the balance of power too much in your favor.

But some other reporters—including those working for smaller news organizations, for trade publications, or in the entertainment press—are often willing to share their questions in advance, allowing you to think through your answers before the interview begins. In either case, reporters are entitled to ask unscripted follow-up questions, so prepare for the interview as if you hadn't seen their inquiries at all.

TAPE THE INTERVIEW

I generally advise against recording your more straightforward interviews, since taping can create a defensive environment before you even begin.

But you may consider audio and/or videotaping your raw interviews with reporters in certain circumstances, especially those you expect to become hostile. Reporters who know you're taping them may take greater care to avoid misquoting you. And if you're misquoted anyway, you can release the raw tape to the public and highlight the reporter's bad behavior. Since many states require you to notify the other party that you're recording, be sure to check the law in your state. Better yet, just tell the reporters they'll be recorded.

LIMIT THE TIME OF THE INTERVIEW

Limiting the time of an interview can prevent it from turning into a harmful fishing expedition. If you believe a journalist is primarily interested in digging for dirt, tell the reporter you'd love to talk but only have a 15-minute window available. Make sure you set the time limit when you are *arranging,* not *conducting* the interview; otherwise, it will look defensive.

Although limiting the time can be a useful tool in certain situations, make it the exception to the rule rather than your standard operating procedure. Your goal is to forge productive relationships with reporters, not to view them as the enemy.

SECTION TWO

Messages And Message Supports

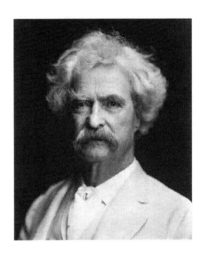

*"I am sorry for such a long letter.
I didn't have time to write a short one."*

Mark Twain

9 WHAT IS A MESSAGE?

Best-selling author and marketing expert Seth Godin estimates that the average American is barraged with 1 million marketing messages each year.

That's about 3,000 per day.

But that figure only includes marketing messages, not messages delivered by media spokespersons in news stories.

So let's call it 3,100 per day.

Now consider the average American. He or she holds down a full-time job, looks after two children, tries to maintain a few social obligations, and suffers from a chronic lack of sleep. That over-scheduled person has almost no time for messages about *anything* to seep in.

Despite that challenge, successful spokespersons regularly manage to cut through the clutter and deliver a message that reaches—and resonates with—those exhausted people. This section of the book will help you craft messages that allow you to do exactly that.

A message is a one-sentence statement that incorporates two things: one of *your* most important points and one of *your audience's* most important needs or values.

Messages often include a call to action, in which the audience is asked to do something specific, such as sign a petition, visit a website, or buy a product.

Aim for three main messages. Three is widely regarded as the right balance between too few (leading to audience boredom) and too many (leading to low audience retention).

This book focuses on messaging for general audiences, but you can also develop more tailored messages for specific audiences (such as potential donors, prospective customers, a crucial voting bloc) using the same technique you'll learn in the next several lessons. Although your messages for each individual audience may differ from the ones you create for your general audience, they should all reflect similar values and themes.

You will probably not use your messages verbatim in media interviews very often; rather, you will communicate the *themes* of your messages in your own words. But since messaging forms the foundation of everything you communicate—in the media, during public presentations, on your website, in brochures, and even during casual conversations—it is important to invest time in developing powerful messages up front.

Messages are not the same as slogans; they are fully formed one-sentence ideas:

> *"By investing in infrastructure today, we will create hundreds of thousands of jobs, resuscitate the manufacturing sector, and build world-class highways that last for generations."*

In contrast, slogans are bumper-sticker or advertising phrases that contain only a few words:

"Rebuilding America, One Brick at a Time"

You will find several more sample messages in lesson 15.

All effective messaging should contain five critical elements, which are summed up by the acronym CUBE A. The next five lessons will discuss the components of CUBE A: Consistent, Unburdened, Brief, Ear-Worthy, and Audience Focused.

10 CUBE A: C IS FOR CONSISTENT

Finish these famous advertising jingles: *

"Like a good neighbor, _____ _____ is there."

"GE: We bring good things ____ _____."

"The best part of wakin' up is _____ in your cup."

Did you find yourself singing along? If so, you've just experienced the first part of CUBE A, which requires that all messages be consistent.

You remember those commercials because the advertisers—State Farm, General Electric, and Folgers—stuck with their catchy ads long enough for them to become almost universally known.

Like memorable commercials, good messages require consistency and repetition. Spokespersons who change their messages from interview to interview prevent their audiences from understanding, remembering, and acting upon their messages, which usually require numerous exposures to become effective.

Just how many times do you have to repeat your messages in order to achieve your goals? Advertisers rely on the concept of *effective frequency* to determine the number of times they should run an advertisement. Commercials for simple products with high name recognition might need to be seen only twice to result in a sales increase, whereas ads for less familiar brands might need to be seen nine times.

In the age of media and message oversaturation, those numbers strike me as low. I advise my clients that moving their audiences from unawareness to action requires anywhere from 7 to 15 exposures— and sometimes more.

Consistency is broader than just media interviews—you should apply it across all of your communications platforms. Your website, public speeches, newsletters, annual reports, and all other internal and external communications should reflect the same themes as your media messages.

Think about it this way: every time a member of your audience hears a consistent message from you, your clicker goes up one notch on your march to 7 to 15 exposures. If I read your on-message quote in a newspaper article, you're at one. If I visit your website and see it again, you're at two. If I see your on-message interview on the local television news, you're at three. But if your message is slightly different each time you communicate, you will never move the clicker past one.

Repeating your main messages may sound confining, but it's not. In a few lessons, you will learn how to keep your messages fresh by reinforcing them with new stories and the latest statistics.

FROM *THE AUDACITY TO WIN* BY DAVID PLOUFFE, BARACK OBAMA'S 2008 CAMPAIGN MANAGER:

"We live in a busy and fractured world in which people are bombarded with pleas for their attention. Given this, you have to try extra hard to reach them. You need to be everywhere. And for people you reach multiple times through different mediums, you need to make sure your message is consistent, so for instance, they don't see a TV ad on tax cuts, hear a radio ad on health care, and click on an Internet ad about energy all on the same day. Messaging needs to be aligned at every level: between offline and on-, principal and volunteer, phone and e-mail."

Answers: State Farm; "to life"; Folgers

11 CUBE A: U IS FOR UNBURDENED

Memory studies consistently find that people forget the vast majority of what they read, hear, or see, especially if they are only exposed to the information one time.

One early study by Herman Ebbinghaus, the 19th-century German psychologist who was among the first to study human memory, found that people forget most of what they learn within days. Although his pioneering research was conducted more than a century ago, it still rings true for those of us who can never quite remember where we left our car keys.

The "U" in CUBE A demands that your messages remain unburdened by three things: wordiness, jargon, and abstractions. The more a message tries to say—and the more abstractly it tries to say it—the less likely it is to be memorable.

As a general guide, aim for messages that:

- Have no more than two commas

- Contain no more than 30 words

- Evoke concrete images

Too many words: Resist the temptation to jam everything you can into a single message—omitting less important details makes good sense. After all, if editors are only going to include two of your quotes in a finished news story, don't you want them to choose your two most important messages? If the editor decides to run your fourth and seventh most important messages instead, I'd question whether your interview was a success.

Technical jargon: Unburdened messages require you to throw jargon overboard. Our clients in technical fields—such as scientists, physicians, and engineers—are the worst offenders of this rule. In fairness, their professional lives are spent awash in technical gobbledygook, their office conversations littered with words rarely used and barely understood by the general public. But considering that the public suffers from information overload, any words that prevent people from quickly grasping your meaning will result in messages that are quickly forgotten.

Even if you think your audience will understand more complicated terms as long as you use them "in context," don't use them (or at least *define* them if you do). They won't hear the end of your sentence if they're still trying to process the unfamiliar word you uttered at the beginning.

AN ACTUAL QUOTE FROM A REAL PRESS RELEASE

"The gradualness (oriented primarily towards actual users) of the new Handy Backup is the succession of interfaces. With all the maximal simplicity and refined usability, the new one is designed to look structurally associative to the previous version..."

Abstractions: Abstractions, or broad concepts or ideas, are difficult for people to visualize. "Justice," for example, is an abstraction—just *try* instantly conjuring up a detailed image of that word. A more concrete message about justice might mention the need to punish thieves who rob old ladies by imprisoning them for the next 20 years. That type of concrete message is much more memorable, and therefore works better for media messaging than an abstract one does. Chip and Dan Heath, the authors of the excellent book *Made to Stick*, write that "trying to teach an abstract principle without concrete foundations is like trying to start a house by building a roof in the air."

The goal of most communications is to move an audience from lack of awareness to awareness to action. The more unburdened your messages, the more likely you are to achieve that goal.

12 CUBE A: B IS FOR BRIEF

During our message development workshops, we help our clients develop three one-sentence messages.

Invariably, someone asks if they can add a second sentence to one of their messages. The person asks the question in the belief that their work is more complicated than that of most other groups, therefore requiring a more detailed explanation.

My answer is always the same: "No."

Writers of newspaper headlines can summarize the world's most consequential topics (domestic terrorism, international warfare, global health pandemics) in just a few words. If they can effectively communicate such complex matters using nothing more than a short phrase, surely our clients can articulate a main message in a single sentence.

The "B" in CUBE A, therefore, demands that your messages remain brief.

How brief? One study from Harvard's Center for Media and Public Affairs found that the average quote airing on evening newscasts lasts just 7.3 seconds. Since most of us speak an average of two or three words per second, that translates to a measly 18 words per quote. I'll cut you a little slack. Aim for no more than 30 words in each of your three messages.

Although the Harvard study focused on television news, the same need for brevity exists for the print media. Next time you read a newspaper, count the number of words in each quote. You'll probably find that each quote runs somewhere between 8 and 20 words.

Before you dismiss the news media as shallow for running such short blurbs, consider their rationale. Excluding commercials, a half-hour television news broadcast lasts just 22 minutes. Minus sports and weather, the program might have 14 minutes left for news. That allows time for just seven two-minute stories, most of which require a set-up, a close, and an opposition voice. No wonder they only have 7.3 seconds for your quote!

Most people find it frustrating to reduce their three main messages to just three sentences. Don't despair. Frustration is an important part of the process, and your disciplined self-editing will result in stronger, more effective messages that stand a greater chance of breaking through and reaching your audience.

I learned that lesson as a young staffer at ABC's *Nightline With Ted Koppel*. After completing my first 16-paragraph feature for the *Nightline* website, my senior producer told me to cut it in half. When I presented him with the eight-paragraph version, he told me it was better—and to cut it in half again. I hated him for making me go through that exercise, but he was right. Four paragraphs were better than eight; eight were better than sixteen. That same lesson holds true for your messages.

CASE STUDY: "DEATH" TAX VS. "ESTATE" TAX

Can you communicate something of meaning in just one sentence? Yes, and pollster Frank Luntz goes even further, suggesting you can be effective with one *word*.

In his book *Words That Work*, Mr. Luntz describes his work to help Republicans eliminate the estate tax, which taxed people who inherited a windfall from a wealthy relative.

He found that while Americans didn't support the abolition of an "estate" tax, which evoked images of sprawling landscapes and mega-mansions, they did support the elimination of the "death" tax, which struck many Americans as inherently unfair. Proponents of its repeal adopted the phrase "death tax" and won the debate.

13 CUBE A: E IS FOR EAR-WORTHY

Before I trained the top spokespersons of one government agency, their public affairs team drafted a few messages for them. The messages were full of seemingly endless sentences that read well enough on paper (sort of), but were almost impossible to speak aloud during media interviews.

I changed this example slightly to protect the client's confidentiality, but the complexity of the message remains intact:

> *"This multilateral agreement, and its steady progress forward, is critical because it will protect Americans who could otherwise be maimed or killed should they consume— knowingly or unknowingly—unapproved imported meats, unpasteurized dairy products, or dangerous unregulated alcoholic beverages."*

Now that you've read that message, go back and speak it aloud.

Since you probably don't speak that formally in everyday conversation, you shouldn't during media interviews, either. (If you still do so by the time you finish *The Media Training Bible*, you might get more value from the book by using it as a doorstop!)

The "E" in CUBE A is for "ear-worthy." The above message fails because it was written for the eye, not the ear.

Below is an alternate version of that message; try speaking this one aloud:

> *"We need to sign this agreement quickly to protect Americans from dangerous meats, dairy products, and alcoholic beverages."*

The above sentence is written for the ear, and most speakers can deliver it in a much more natural manner.

Here are five tips to help you write for the ear:

1. **Use short words:** Big words sound impressive. But multisyllabic words are rarely as good as their simpler counterparts when writing for the ear.

> *"Short words are the best and old words when short are the best of all." – Winston Churchill*

2. **Use short sentences:** Short sentences are more impactful than longer ones. The first example on the previous page has 39 words; the second has just 18. There's a good reason the most memorable lines from famous speeches rarely exceed 20 words.

3. **Use everyday words:** One fascinating study found that adults can understand 96 percent of all spoken English with a vocabulary of just 2,000 words. Although most native English speakers know thousands more, they tend to use a rather limited pool of words in conversation. When speaking to general audiences, you should too.

> *"I never write 'metropolis' for seven cents, because I can get the same price for 'city.' I never write 'policeman,' because I can get the same money for 'cop.'" – Mark Twain*

4. **Use contractions:** Barring the most formal speeches, oral delivery usually benefits from the use of contractions. "Do not" and "they are" work best for the eye. "Don't" and "they're" work best for the ear.

5. **Speak messages aloud:** When you finish drafting your messages, read them aloud. If any of them contain a word that doesn't roll easily off your tongue, replace it with a shorter and simpler one that does.

14 CUBE A: A IS FOR AUDIENCE FOCUSED

According to Oxford Online, the most popular pronoun in the English language is "I." That means if *I* listen to your message, *I'll* need to know how *I* will be affected to determine whether *I* should act or if *I* even care.

So you may have noticed a small problem after reading the first four parts of CUBE A: They're all about you, not your audience.

The "A" in CUBE A helps ensure that your message is "audience focused." Effective media messages must incorporate your audience's *needs* and *values*; those that do will resonate much more deeply.

Needs refer to things people require or desire. In the 1940s, psychologist Abraham Maslow identified the most common human requirements in his "Hierarchy of Needs." Human needs, he said, include safety and security, family and friendship, health, confidence, respect by others, and love. In today's fast-moving world, I would add time, work-life balance, and convenience to his list.

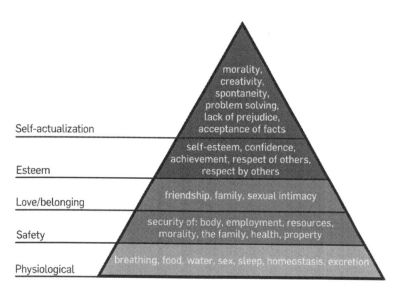

Maslow's Hierarchy of Needs

30

Values refer to the guiding principles people and communities share, including patriotism, compassion or aggression, and self-reliance or collaboration.

Most values are subjective. For example, churchgoers believe in a higher power while atheists lack religious faith. Yet they both share the conviction that *their* values are correct. Those types of disagreements about which values are "right" drive political and social argument, something you see on display in debates and television commercials every four years during presidential campaign season.

For media messaging, the perfect marriage exists somewhere between *your goals* and *your audience's needs and values.*

CASE STUDY: IBM PRESS RELEASE

I expected the worst when I came across a press release with this headline: "Southeast Texas Medical Associates Building Strong Post Treatment Care Programs with IBM Business Analytics Software."

To my surprise, the release wasn't a self-indulgent and product-focused pitch, but rather an audience-focused announcement framed within the needs of patients:

"Each day we challenge ourselves to respond faster, more efficiently and more effectively to the needs of our patients. You'd be surprised at the demand we get from our patients; they expect us to not just treat their ailments today, but to help them put plans in place to tackle ailments and challenges they will eventually face when dealing with a chronic disease like diabetes," said Dr. James Holly, CEO, Southeast Texas Medical Associates.

This message succeeds because it isn't about IBM's software, but instead what that software can do for you.

15 TYPES OF MESSAGES

There are many different types of media messages, but they frequently fit within one of the following four categories:

1. Fact/Result

2. Problem/Solution

3. Advocacy or Call to Action

4. Benefits

In the messages below, you'll notice overlap among the categories. That's because the same message can usually be written many different ways, depending on your goals.

1. THE FACT/RESULT MESSAGE

This message spells out the link between a fact and its implication.

> *"Pennsylvania's unreasonable malpractice laws have resulted in thousands of pregnant women living more than 100 miles from their obstetricians, a potentially life-threatening distance during medical emergencies."*

> *"Children in low-income communities receive a much poorer education than children from wealthier areas, and are too often doomed to a lifetime of low-paying jobs as a result."*

2. THE PROBLEM/SOLUTION MESSAGE

This type of message describes the problem in the first clause and its solution in the second; that formula can also be reversed.

> *"Sterling Lake has become badly polluted and is no longer safe for swimming or fishing, but by closing it for three years, we can restore it and open it for swimming and fishing again."*

"By loosening Pennsylvania's unreasonable malpractice laws, thousands of pregnant women will be able to find a local obstetrician who can help in case of a medical emergency."

3. THE ADVOCACY OR CALL-TO-ACTION MESSAGE

This kind of message goes a step further than the previous ones, providing your audience with a specific call to action.

"Call your state senators and tell them to pass this bill so that pregnant women no longer have to drive 100 miles to visit their obstetrician."

"More American workers are living in dire poverty than at any other time since the early 1900s, so I'd ask everyone listening to sign our petition to Congress demanding a fair minimum wage at (www.insertwebsiteaddresshere.com)."

4. THE BENEFITS MESSAGE

Benefits messages focus on selling points for potential buyers.

"We are taking the hassles out of air travel by offering passengers the airline they've long wanted, with free itinerary changes, more legroom, and Internet access."

"Using our print-on-demand service, our customers can upload their work on Thursday and have it bound and delivered on Friday—for half the price of traditional printers."

When you begin crafting your three messages in the next lesson, mix and match these message types. For example, a nonprofit organization might use two problem/solution messages along with a call-to-action one, while a small business might use a fact/result message, a problem/solution message, and a benefits message. If you're stuck, create four versions of each message to determine which one helps you accomplish your goals best.

16 EXERCISE: CRAFT YOUR MESSAGES

This lesson will focus on crafting three winning messages about your company or organization for the general public. You can also use the same technique to develop more specific messages for individual topics or campaigns, or for different audiences.

If you create messages for individual topics or campaigns, remember that those messages should also reinforce your *overall* organizational messages.

For example, a women's health nonprofit might have three overall messages: one that emphasizes treatment, another that focuses on prevention, and a third about research. The group may also have numerous specialty areas, such as neonatal health, breast cancer, and bone loss. The messages about a specific specialty area, say breast cancer, should help reinforce the overall messages about the importance of treatment, prevention, and/or research.

STEP ONE: WHAT *YOU* WANT

What are the most important things the public needs to know about your organization's work? Begin typing some ideas. Don't be self-critical—just brainstorm and type anything (a word, a phrase, a sentence) that comes to mind. When you've run out of gas, save and close the document. Come back a few days later with fresh eyes and add anything you might have missed.

When you're satisfied that you've fully completed your brainstorming, select the three thoughts that represent what you *most* want the public to know about your organization's work. Write them out in sentence form as three separate messages, similar to the examples provided in the previous lesson. Don't be discouraged if you aren't creating perfect messages immediately—you're aiming for a starting point, not perfection.

STEP TWO: WHAT *THEY* NEED

Put your messages aside for a while. Open a fresh document and brainstorm everything you can about what the general public wants or needs from you.

Let's say you were part of the group trying to help pregnant women in Pennsylvania. While brainstorming what the general public wants related to that issue, you might have said:

1. They want to protect the health of mother and child.

2. They want to ensure easy access to obstetricians.

3. They want to know that someone is fighting for them.

When you finish brainstorming, select the three items you think your audience wants or needs from you most. Then, pull out your messages. Are those three needs represented in your messages? If so, you're finished. If not, edit your messages to articulate them within the context of what your audience needs.

As an example, consider this message:

> *"By loosening Pennsylvania's unreasonable malpractice laws, thousands of pregnant women will be able to find a local obstetrician who can help in case of a medical emergency."*

That message reflects the first two audience needs listed above: to protect the health of mother and child, and to ensure easy access to obstetricians.

STEP THREE: BEGIN YOUR MESSAGE WORKSHEETS

Once you've completed your three messages, turn to lesson 93 and write your messages down, one on each of the three message worksheets provided.

17 WHAT IS A MESSAGE SUPPORT?

Congratulations! You've now created three terrific messages, a significant achievement. Of course, if you simply repeat those three sentences over and over during your next media interview, you'll infuriate the audience and alienate the reporter.

You can easily avoid that fate by using "message supports" to reinforce your messages. There are three types of message supports: stories, statistics, and sound bites. For each of your messages, you should develop at least two of each type of support, which will allow you to articulate the main *themes* of your messages in every answer without ever sounding repetitive.

Message supports can be paired with a message or used on their own. For example, you might answer one question using a message, the next using a message paired with a story, and another using only a statistic.

The key is to make sure that all of your statistics, stories, and sound bites reinforce your messages.

> *There are three types of message supports:*
> *stories, statistics, and sound bites.*

The first two legs of the stool are stories and statistics. When speaking to general audiences, it is important to maintain an equal balance of both—stories will resonate better for some people, while statistics will be more effective for others. As author Frank Luntz notes in his book *Words That Work*:

> *"Women generally respond to stories, anecdotes, and metaphors, while men are more fact-oriented and statistical. Men appreciate a colder, more scientific, almost mathematical approach; women's sensibilities tend to be more personal, human, and literary."*

Although social science indeed suggests that gender helps determine whether a person is more likely to prefer stories or statistics, my personal experience is that a person's profession is a much more accurate indicator. For example, scientists tend to be "statistics" people regardless of gender, while social workers usually lean toward the "stories" side. Therefore, make sure you balance your interviews. If you tend to be a "stories" person, add an extra statistic or two; if you're a "statistics" person, do the opposite.

The third leg of the stool is for "sound bites," those short quips most people *wish* they could think up on the fly. The good news is that most great spokespersons plan their sound bites well in advance—they just *deliver* them as if they were improvised.

The following five lessons will teach you how to dazzle your audiences by using message supports in your next interview.

18 STORIES

According to Howard Gardner, a professor at Harvard University, "Stories are the single most powerful weapon in a leader's rhetorical arsenal." Yet most people struggle to think of compelling stories that reinforce their messages.

That's usually because they're trying to think of a "big" story. In order to help people get unstuck, I tell them to think smaller. I encourage them to think of a single customer whose life was improved because of their product or a community that is enjoying the benefits of a new public school.

A story can be many things: your personal experience with a person, place, thing, or topic; somebody else's experience; case studies in the news; or a historical or fictional example.

Take this message from a few lessons ago:

> *"By investing in infrastructure today, we will create hundreds of thousands of jobs, resuscitate the manufacturing sector, and build world-class highways that last for generations."*

A "story" to go with that message might say:

> *"The owner of one steel factory in Pennsylvania told me that his company is on the verge of bankruptcy, but that this bill would keep his factory open and his 200 workers employed. Plus, he said it would be nice to finally be able to build roads that don't fall apart after every snowstorm!"*

The message itself likely didn't help you create a clear mental picture, but the story probably conjured up images of a factory floor, steelworkers, or potholed roads. Good stories do exactly that: they bring abstract messages to life through more tangible examples.

In *Made to Stick*, authors Chip and Dan Heath identified three types of "story plots" that are most commonly used to energize and inspire others. If you're having a difficult time thinking of stories, these plots may help you brainstorm:

1. **The Challenge Plot:** A protagonist overcomes a challenge and succeeds; examples include David vs. Goliath and rags to riches stories.

2. **The Connection Plot:** A story about people who develop a relationship that bridges a gap; examples include racial, class, ethnic, or demographic differences.

3. **The Creativity Plot:** A person makes a mental breakthrough, solves a long-standing puzzle, or attacks a problem in an innovative way.

CASE STUDY: HURRICANE MITCH STRIKES HONDURAS

When Hurricane Mitch hit Honduras in 1998, thousands of people died and hundreds of thousands were left homeless.

By the time ABC News anchor Ted Koppel made it to the Honduran capital, the magnitude of the hurricane had already been widely reported. He knew a show highlighting the number of deaths wouldn't add much to the story.

While walking around the city, he came across a man holding a shovel in a debris field. Koppel asked what he was digging. "My house used to be here, and it was destroyed," the man said. "But I built the front door of my house with my own hands, and damn it, I want it back."

That poignant moment became the centerpiece of a program called "The Door." The show focused on that man – who he was, what had happened to him, and what he was planning to do next. By telling that small story well, the audience was able to extrapolate and understand the much larger disaster.

19 STATISTICS

Four and a half million Americans have Alzheimer's disease.

Did that number make you think, "Wow!" Did it evoke a specific image of what 4.5 million people looks like? I'm guessing not.

The problem is that most of us can't remember raw numbers or place them into a larger perspective. Yes, the second leg of the message support stool is statistics, but that isn't the same as raw data. Your job is to take boring, impersonal numbers and provide them with meaningful context that elicits a powerful reaction.

For example, imagine you're giving an interview to a Boston radio station. You might cite the Alzheimer's statistic this way:

> *"Fenway Park seats 37,000 people. It would take 122 Fenway Parks to hold every American with Alzheimer's disease. That's four and a half million people in total who are afflicted with this awful disease."*

For most people that statistic, loaded with context, is more powerful. It paints a memorable mental picture and produces a "wow" response. Here are four additional ways to cite statistics:

1. **Make numbers personal:** Numbers are often best when reduced to a personal level. Instead of saying a tax cut would save Americans $100 billion this year, say the average family of four would receive $1,250 in tax relief.

2. **Don't rely on percentages:** Instead of proclaiming that your company's new energy-efficient manufacturing equipment will cut your plant's carbon footprint by 35 percent, be more specific. Will that new efficiency save 20,000 gallons of oil this year, enough to fuel 36 company trucks for an entire year? Say so!

3. **Use ratios:** An estimated 170,000 people in Washington, DC, are functionally illiterate. But that number doesn't tell you much, especially if you have no sense of the overall population. Instead, you might say:

   "One in three adults living in Washington, DC, is functionally illiterate. Next time you're on the Metro, look around you. Odds are that the person to your left or right can't read a newspaper."

4. **Provide relative distance:** If your car company is introducing an updated model, you'd be proud to announce that the improved version gets four miles more per gallon. But you'd get even more traction if you said, "That's enough to get from Maine to Miami once per year—without spending an extra penny on gas."

CASE STUDY: CHRISTIAN CHILDREN'S FUND COMMERCIALS (V)

If you're of a certain age, you probably remember those old television commercials for the Christian Children's Fund. In them, actress Sally Struthers (*All in the Family*) sold viewers the promise of saving a child for "the price of a cup of coffee."

A quarter-century later, those ads are still memorable. And the way Ms. Struthers used numbers in those commercials is a big reason why.

The ads succeeded by reducing numbers down to a manageable price tag for most viewers: "For about 70 cents, you can buy a can of soda....In Ethiopia, for just 70 cents a day, you can feed a child like Jamal nourishing meals."

Imagine if Ms. Struthers had used an annual price tag instead of a daily one by saying, "You can save a child for just $255 a year." Few people would have anted up, and the ads wouldn't be remembered today.

20   WHAT ARE SOUND BITES?

Have you ever noticed that certain media guests seem to have the knack for always coming up with the perfect quip?

It's true that some of those people possess a rare gift for ad-libbing. But for the rest of us, Mark Twain captured it best when he said, "It usually takes about three weeks to prepare a good impromptu speech."

A sound bite is a short phrase or sentence that expresses one of your messages in a particularly memorable or witty manner (they are occasionally slightly longer). The media love sound bites and audiences remember them. They make dull stories livelier and boring guests more interesting.

CASE STUDIES: HISTORY'S "IMPROMPTU" SOUND BITES (V)

Two of the late 20th century's most memorable sound bites were planned well in advance:

O.J. Simpson Trial, 1995: At the O.J. Simpson murder trial, attorney Johnnie Cochran instructed the jury, "If [the glove] doesn't fit, you must acquit." Cochran's line wasn't improvised; it wasn't even his. Another member of Simpson's legal team, Gerald Uelmen, created the sound bite. Either way, that quip was the key to Simpson's acquittal.

Vice-Presidential Debate, 1988: When young Republican VP nominee Dan Quayle defended his preparedness for office by saying he had the same amount of experience as John F. Kennedy, his opponent pounced. "I knew Jack Kennedy," said Democratic VP nominee Lloyd Bentsen. "Jack Kennedy was a friend of mine. Senator, you're no Jack Kennedy."

The crowd cheered enthusiastically at his "improvised" line. But the line wasn't improvised. A clever political consultant created it in advance.

Here are 10 examples of media-friendly sound bites:

> "It's like trying to fill the bathtub with the drain open." – Mary Johnson, Medicare policy analyst

> "Any one flight in space on the space shuttle is as dangerous as 60 combat missions during wartime." – John Young, astronaut

> "We're burning the furniture to heat the house."— John H. Quigley, Pennsylvania Department of Conservation, on hydraulic fracturing

> "She couldn't get elected if two of her opponents died." – Peck Young, political consultant

> "Not only is the president's honeymoon over, he now has a divorce on his hands." – Marshall Wittman, pundit

> "With all the money we owe China, I think we might rightly say, 'Hu's your daddy.'" – Rep. Michele Bachmann (R-MN), referring to Chinese president Hu Jintao

> "I outwit them and then I out hit them." – Muhammad Ali, three-time heavyweight boxing champion

> "Our choices right now are not between good and better; they're between bad and worse." – Alan Greenspan, former chairman of the U.S. Federal Reserve

> "My favorite recent movie is Hereafter. I didn't cry at the end— but I thought about it." – Michael Jordan, former NBA star

> "How many times are we going to gamble with lives, economies, and ecosystems?" – John Hocevar, Greenpeace USA

In the next lesson, you will learn how to create memorable sound bites that will hook the media and the public.

21 HOW TO CREATE SOUND BITES

Few people can compose captivating sound bites in a single sitting. Don't give up. You *can* develop media-friendly sound bites.

Great sound bites are all around you. Listen closely during conversations with friends and colleagues. What are intended as throwaway comments during casual banter often contain a gem worth saving—so keep pen and paper nearby to record the unexpected gold.

Marcia Yudkin, the "Head Stork" of Named At Last, a naming and tagline development company, came up with 17 tips to help spokespersons create memorable sound bites. I highly recommend her ebook *The Sound Bite Workbook.* Among other ideas, she advises spokespersons to brainstorm a list of keywords related to their topic area, look in a thesaurus for unexpected word options, and identify relevant homophones.

Below, you'll find 10 types of sound bites the media regularly quote, along with examples for each. (Thanks to Marcia for her help with this list.)

1. **Similes, Metaphors, and Analogies:** "It's as if Republicans and Democrats are planning a trip, but they disagree over whether you should start the trip from Buenos Aires or Greenland." – Howard Gleckman, Tax Policy Center

2. **Triples:** "We help ordinary people get rich without working on Wall Street, inheriting wealth, or marrying a millionaire."

3. **Rhetorical Questions:** "More than 600,000 Americans lost their jobs last month. How many more families need to lose their economic lifeline before Congress acts?"

4. **Contrasts, Conflicts, or Paradoxes:** "Our food is fresh. Our customers are spoiled." – FreshDirect, online grocer

5. **Definitiveness or Power:** "We are in this to win." – Gen. David Petraeus

6. **Superlatives:** "This is the biggest technological advance in 50 years in the oil business." – Philip Crouse, oil analyst

7. **Pop Culture:** "There's a greater likelihood that I'll be asked by Madonna to go on tour as her bass player than I'll be picked to be on the ticket." – Former Gov. Mike Huckabee (R-AR), assessing his chances of becoming Mitt Romney's vice-presidential running mate in 2012

8. **Emotions:** "As a New Yorker, I am absolutely horrified by what happened in my city last night." – Commenter on Daily Kos website about alleged police brutality at a local protest

9. **Surprise Twist:** "I will not exploit, for political purposes, my opponent's youth and inexperience." – President Ronald Reagan, diffusing accusations that he was too old for a second term

10. **Tweaked Clichés:** "Money doesn't grow on trees, but it does grow faster in credit unions without those greedy big-bank fees."

EXERCISE: COMPLETE YOUR MESSAGE WORKSHEETS

Turn to lesson 93, where you should have already written down your three main messages. Brainstorm at least two stories, statistics, and sound bites that reinforce each of your three messages, and write them in your worksheets.

22 USING MESSAGE SUPPORTS DURING AN INTERVIEW

This lesson will illustrate how the individual pieces you've created—your messages and message supports (stories, statistics, and sound bites)—fit together.

You may remember this message, about the risks pregnant women in Pennsylvania face, from lesson 15:

> "By loosening Pennsylvania's unreasonable malpractice laws, thousands of pregnant women will be able to find a local obstetrician who can help in case of a medical emergency."

A story that would fit beneath that message might say:

> "Jane Jackson, a 26-year-old from Altoona, was in her seventh month of pregnancy last year when she went into labor. She was by herself and called 9-1-1. The paramedics got there in time but didn't have the skills to help when her baby was unable to breathe. Her baby son died. If her skilled obstetrician lived closer, he likely would have been able to save her baby."

A statistic under that message might be:

> "More than 18,000 women of childbearing age in Pennsylvania live at least 100 miles from the closest obstetrician."

A sound bite supporting that message might read:

> "Having your doctor 100 miles away is kind of like keeping your Band-Aids at a friend's house—they're useless when you need them most."

The sample interview on the next page shows you how to embed your messages and message supports seamlessly into every answer.

SAMPLE INTERVIEW

Question 1: Why is there a shortage of obstetricians in Pennsylvania, and what is your group trying to do about it?

Answer: There's a shortage because our state's unreasonable malpractice laws are chasing doctors away. We're trying to loosen those overly restrictive laws. Doing so would allow thousands of pregnant women to find a local obstetrician who can help in case of a medical emergency."

Question 2: How big of a problem is this in Pennsylvania?

Answer: It's a huge problem. You know, I met a 26-year-old woman recently who was in her seventh month of pregnancy last year when she went into early labor. The paramedics got there in time but didn't have the skills to help when her baby was unable to breathe. Her son died, and he probably would have survived if her skilled obstetrician worked nearby. I'm hearing far too many of those stories lately, and we need to change these malpractice laws immediately to prevent any more of these tragedies from taking place.

Question 3: What do you say to those who believe that it's a good idea to keep tough malpractice laws in place?

Answer: I would remind them that more than 18,000 women of childbearing age in Pennsylvania live at least 100 miles from the closest obstetrician, which places them at great risk. Having your doctor an hour away is kind of like keeping your Band-Aids at a friend's house—they're useless when you need them most. It's a dangerous and sometimes life-threatening situation, and something has to change.

In question one, the spokesperson answered using a message. For question two, the spokesperson began with a story and then transitioned back to the message. To answer the third question, the spokesperson used a statistic followed by a sound bite.

SECTION THREE

The Interview

"The best way to be boring is to leave nothing out."

Voltaire, French writer and philosopher

23 REPEAT, REPEAT, REPEAT

We've all seen those politicians on television who keep reciting the same message points over and over again.

Such overt repetition tends to infuriate the audience. It's easy to picture viewers rolling their eyes in disgust and shouting, "Answer the question!" at their television sets—*if* they didn't already flip to a different channel.

As a result, the politicians not only fail to persuade the audience but also diminish their reputations in the process.

So it may surprise you that my advice is to articulate a message or message support in almost *every answer you ever give.*

> *You should articulate a message or message support in almost every answer you ever give.*

I don't mean that you should repeat the same words in every answer, but rather that all of your answers should convey the *theme* of at least one of your main messages.

If you filled in the message worksheets in lesson 93, you now have 21 different answers: three in the form of messages, six as stories, six as statistics, and six as sound bites. Those 21 answers allow you to answer 21 different questions in 21 different ways, all of which are "on message" but none of which are repetitive.

You may occasionally wonder whether it's okay to abandon your message for an answer or two along the way. I'd encourage you not to. Here's why: Let's say a newspaper reporter asks you 10 questions during an interview. You articulate a message or message support in 7 of your 10 answers. Pretty good, right?

But what happens if the reporter chooses to quote one of your other three answers? It means your one quote in the story—that one critical opportunity to influence or educate your audience— will not contain one of your most important points.

I know that may sound obvious, but I can count dozens of exasperated clients who have asked me at some point, "Why did the reporter include that quote? It wasn't even that important!" I always respond the same way: "If you don't want it quoted, don't say it at all."

I often joke with my clients that you should even transition to a message when a reporter asks, "How are you?" I'm kidding, but barely. Most questions are opportunities to communicate a message or message support, so don't waste any answers. Today's wasted answer may become tomorrow's quote.

> *Don't waste any answers. Today's wasted answer may become tomorrow's quote.*

Unless the interview is live, reporters will usually offer you a final opportunity to get your messages out. Journalists typically end their interviews by asking if they missed anything or whether there's anything you'd like to add. Seize that opportunity. If you said everything you needed to say during the interview, restate a key point. If you forgot to state one of your messages, that's the perfect time to do it.

Finally, remember to treat your communications with reporters before and after the interview as if they're part of the "official" interview. Your interactions with reporters prior to an interview may help inform the questions they ask, and your follow-up emails may help the reporter remember to include a key point in the final story.

24 DON'T EDUCATE THE REPORTER

My firm has offices in New York City and Washington, DC, so I frequently take the train between the two cities. On one such trip, I overheard a PR professional speaking to a colleague.

"The reporter from the *Philadelphia Daily News* completely blew the story," she said, clearly infuriated. "I talked to him *forever,* and he totally missed the point!"

I immediately wondered whether the problem was that she had said too much—and by doing so, might have obscured her message.

Too often, media spokespersons fall victim to the "tell them everything you know" syndrome. They wrongly believe that their primary role in an interview is to provide the reporter with an in-depth education instead of remembering that their main goal is to influence the story and get the quotes they want.

Sure, providing reporters with the information they need in order to file a story is an important part of your job as a spokesperson. But the more detail you provide, the more likely a secondary or tertiary point will make its way into the story instead of a primary one.

Put another way, a media interview isn't about downloading your knowledge—it's about *prioritizing* your knowledge. As we tell our clients, the more you say, the more you stray.

I'll be even a bit more provocative here: Your main task as a spokesperson isn't to give the reporter facts. If you merely spout facts, you'll be no more valuable than a Wikipedia entry. Your job is to give those facts *context* and *meaning.*

When speaking to print reporters in person, you'll probably observe them furiously scribbling notes in a small notepad. In order to capture everything, they usually write in big, barely legible characters and flip the pages at an almost manic pace. By the end of the interview, reporters may have dozens of pages of notes.

If you remain focused on your most critical points, you will help reporters prioritize. They may walk away with 12 pages of notes, but your clarity will make it easy for them to immediately identify your three most important themes. That doesn't guarantee they'll use them—but it dramatically increases the probability they will.

Alternatively, if you're not focused enough, you will give the reporter 12 pages' worth of random, unprioritized thoughts from which to choose. If you're fortunate enough to get the quote you wanted, it would be due more to luck than design.

There's an easy way to know if you're abandoning your main messages. If you ever say the following phrases during an interview (or anything similar), you've probably wandered pretty far off message:

- "Oh, by the way…"

- "Incidentally…"

- "As an aside…"

- "That reminds me of something else…"

I suspect that's where the woman on the train went wrong. As she said, she "talked to him forever," almost certainly meaning her answers were unprioritized. She likely gave the reporter 12 pages' worth of unfocused notes, forcing him to choose what to include. And, as usually happens in that circumstance, she was unhappy with the result.

She forgot that her primary job was not to educate but to prioritize.

25   TALK SHORT, BUT NOT *TOO* SHORT

If you've ever been deposed in a legal case, your attorney probably instructed you to answer questions using the fewest number of words possible. In a legal setting, saying too much can come back to haunt you. So when you're asked if you know what time it is during a deposition, the correct answer isn't "half past one," but "yes."

No wonder attorneys often make the worst media guests. They end their answers abruptly, leaving the audience to wonder why their answers sound so artificially clipped and carefully parsed.

The attorneys who bring their best legal advice to media interviews— "Say only what you *have* to say, then stop"—are missing one critical ingredient. Unlike legal depositions, media interviews represent an opportunity to advocate more fully for your product or idea.

The proper advice is this: "Say what you have to say, briefly advocate for your product or idea, and *then* stop." You can advocate using a combination of your messages, message supports, and/or a call to action.

As you read earlier, the average quote from media spokespersons on evening newscasts is just 7.3 seconds, an average of 18 words. But that doesn't mean you need to answer every question in 7.3 seconds. Sure, it's helpful if your answers are short and tight. But it's even more important to ensure that each of your sentences expresses a complete thought and can stand on its own. That way, it doesn't matter which sentence a reporter chooses—if everything you say reflects one of your main messages, a message support, or a call to action, then *anything* the reporter prints will be "on message."

For example, you may remember this answer from a few lessons ago:

> *I would remind people that more than 18,000 women of childbearing age in Pennsylvania live at least 100 miles from the closest obstetrician, which places them at great risk.*

Having your doctor an hour away is like keeping your Band-Aids at a friend's house—they're useless when you need them most. It's a life-threatening situation, and something has to change."

That answer contains three sentences, but it doesn't matter which of them the reporter chooses to quote. Any of the three would serve as an on-message response.

That doesn't mean you have license to drone on. Aim to keep your answers to no more than about 30 seconds in length. But you're allowed to give a more complete answer than you would be advised to deliver at trial.

CASE STUDY: BILL CLINTON GOES ON JOHNNY CARSON

Before he ran for president in 1992, Bill Clinton was best known for his 1988 nominating speech at the Democratic National Convention, which droned on for an hour.

Viewers who saw the speech all those years ago probably don't remember a word he said, but they likely remember the television cutaways showing delegates of his own party nodding off. And they probably remember the restless crowd cheering when he finally uttered the words, "And in conclusion."

A few nights later, Mr. Clinton appeared on *The Tonight Show Starring Johnny Carson*. Carson's first question? "So, Governor, how are you?" Without pausing, Carson reached under his desk, pulled out an hourglass, and turned it upside down.

The audience roared.

26 THE REPORTER ISN'T YOUR AUDIENCE

At the beginning of a media interview, many spokespersons remember to answer questions using their messages and message supports. But as the interview progresses and begins to resemble a normal, everyday conversation, they suddenly forget to include their messages.

That's dangerous not only for the reasons you've already read, but also because it usually means they're directing their answers to the reporter, not their audience.

A media interview is not a conversation with a reporter. It is a highly focused form of communication aimed squarely at your audience. The reporter is merely the conduit through which you reach it. That doesn't mean you should ignore reporters, but rather that you should focus your communication on the people you're trying to reach.

As an example, I occasionally receive a negative comment on our blog from someone who disagrees with something I've written. If I'm nasty in my response, the entire audience will hold it against me. If I treat the person with respect (in some cases, more than they deserve), readers are more likely to be impressed with the tone of my reply—even if they, too, disagree.

Therefore, I try to remember that the writer of that letter is not my target audience. Sure, my response is *addressed* to the commenter, but my communication is really intended for the rest of the blog's readers. So beware of slipping into a conversation with the reporter. If you do, you'll be speaking with the commenter rather than to the readers.

Here are three ways to make sure you're directing your communication to your audience:

1. **Visualize a member of your audience:** Most people find the idea of speaking to 100,000 people through a reporter absolutely terrifying. The good news is that you never have to fear a large audience again. Instead, visualize one specific person

in your target audience that you need to reach in order to be successful. Be specific. Focus your answers on that one individual. If that person understands what you're saying, odds are the rest of your audience will too.

For one interview, one of our clients visualized that his "target person" was a retired 78-year-old African American woman living by herself in rural Nevada. He further defined her by saying she retired nine years ago after working as a trauma nurse for 40 years. By being that specific, he was able to visualize that woman during his entire interview, helping him reach the *entire* audience more effectively.

Before reading further, take a moment to identify and visualize your target person.

2. **Base your interview on the audience's level of knowledge:** If you're speaking about climate change with a reporter who has covered that issue for a decade, you might be tempted to speak at a higher level by using acronyms or technical jargon. Don't. The reporter isn't your audience; the person you visualized is. Speak to the reporter as you would to your target person.

3. **Don't call reporters by name:** Many media trainers teach their trainees to call reporters by their names, arguing that doing so helps forge a warm connection with the interviewer. Perhaps that's true. But it comes at too high of a price. When you call reporters by name, it makes it clear to the audience that you're speaking to the reporter, not with them. (More on this in lesson 67.)

27 THE 12-YEAR-OLD-NEPHEW RULE

"Oh, so you want me to dumb it down."

If there's one sentence that makes my skin crawl, that is it. When a trainee says those words, I occasionally respond with this:

> *"We have to drop a SOT and a VO into the package and get it on the bird."*

They look at me with a quizzical expression until I explain what that piece of television jargon means:

> *"I have to insert a sound bite and a voiceover into the news segment I'm working on and then send it by satellite to another bureau."*

Did I "dumb down" the phrase, or just strip it of jargon and put it into plain English? I'd argue I did the latter, and it's not a small distinction. "Dumbing down" is a phrase that views your audience as an object of condescension, whereas "simplifying it" connotes respect for your audience.

Simplified communication will allow you to reach the six in ten American adults who haven't obtained an associate's degree and the one in five Americans who speak a foreign language at home and may not speak fluent English.

This comes up frequently when I deal with scientists, academics, and others in technical fields. They understandably value the nuance in their work, and they bristle at the idea of simplifying information at the risk of making it inaccurate.

But there's usually a middle ground between nuance and inaccuracy, and a quote often attributed to Albert Einstein gets it exactly right: "Everything should be made as simple as possible, but not simpler." There's just no reason for a spokesperson to say "consortium" instead of "partnership," or "rapid intensification" instead of "quickly getting worse."

Even when you speak to more sophisticated audiences—perhaps through a trade journal or industry publication—there *still* may be important people in your audience who aren't familiar with industry buzzwords, so there's little harm in simplifying your communication. Here are three tips to help you eliminate jargon:

1. **The 12-Year-Old-Nephew Rule:** A former ABC News colleague of mine once interviewed a jargon-spouting scientist. After 20 minutes, the scientist still hadn't said anything we could use on air. She ended the interview, thanked him, and said, "Could I ask you a favor? My 12-year-old nephew loves science. Would you mind doing a take I could show to him?" He agreed and delivered a terrific answer without any jargon—and that's the quote we used that evening. If you have young people in your life, run your messages by them. If they can paraphrase them in their own words, you've successfully eliminated the jargon.

2. **Tell yourself you don't get it:** I often help people eliminate jargon by interrupting them during an answer and saying, "I'm sorry, I'm not sure I get it." Their next attempt is usually simpler, but not perfect. So I'll try again: "I'm sorry. I'm still not sure I understand." They almost always land on a simpler response within a few attempts—which means for the first time, they finally have a broadly understandable, media-friendly answer.

3. **If you have to use a technical term, define it:** You may occasionally need to use a technical term or acronym. Just make sure you briefly define it. For taped interviews, define the term every time you say it since you don't know which answer the reporter will use. For live interviews, define it on every second or third mention. That may seem like overkill, but since some people will tune into your interview in the middle, they'll have no idea what the word means if you don't define it again.

28 USE STRONG LANGUAGE

An exasperated President Harry Truman once quipped, "Give me a one-handed economist. All my economists say, 'On the one hand, on the other!'" Like Truman's economists, too many media spokespersons hedge their statements with weak words, burying important content in the language of uncertainty.

For example, consider the contrast between these two quotes:

> *Version 1: "We think there are a lot of important charities that people can contribute to, but we hope that people will give to ours, since we believe we are providing an important service for Cincinnati's homeless population."*

> *Version 2: "Cincinnati's homeless have fewer shelters available to them than at any other time in the past 30 years, and we're asking all local residents to make a donation immediately to make sure our city's homeless have the warm shelter and food they need to survive this cold winter."*

The first version fails because it is dominated by the language of uncertainty—"we think," "we hope," and "we believe." Quote two, on the other hand, uses strong phrases and words such as, "at any other time," "immediately," and "need."

Spokespersons working in technical fields are notorious for their never-ending use of hedged language. Afraid to say anything definitive, they water down their messages into a tentative mush that ends up saying nothing at all.

In fairness, their concerns are real. Scientists, economists, and policy analysts worry about the implications of being inaccurate in their media statements—and they know they'll receive a disapproving look from their colleagues if they leave out a critical detail. Plus, they worry that incorrect statements could be used against them in future media stories.

But spokespersons waffle more than they need to, unnecessarily reducing the impact of their communication. Their hedging may even cost them their chance to be included in news stories at all, since journalists are inclined to drop sources who won't express a clear viewpoint.

To eliminate unnecessary tentative language, focus on the parts of your story that *are* 100 percent true. Three examples of absolute language follow; I've bolded the declarative words:

1. You might not be able to say that a new drug will work, but you could say it's the **most promising** new drug you've seen in your career.

2. You might not be able to say that your company has never had a safety violation, but you could say you've **never had** a major incident at your plant.

3. You might not be able to say that your nonprofit's fundraising drive will solve the problem, but you could say that **more** people in your community have volunteered to help **than ever before**.

Here are a few weak phrases and their stronger counterparts:

TENTATIVE	STRONG
"We may"	"Here's what we're committed to"
"I think"	"Here's what we know"
"It seems"	"It's clear that"
"We're trying"	"We are doing"
"We believe "	"The evidence tells us"

29 DON'T BURY THE LEAD: START AT THE END

Everything you know about telling a story is wrong.

Did that provocative opening statement grab your attention? I'm guessing it did. But most media spokespersons don't speak that way. They want to tell a more complete story, losing their audience's attention before they finally arrive at their main point. Most people begin with something like this:

> *"At a very early age, most of us are taught how to tell stories using a chronological sentence structure—beginning, middle, and end. While that narrative structure works well in some contexts, it does not work particularly well for media interviews. My goal is to teach media spokespersons how to begin with their lead—or most important point—instead of relying on an imperfect and ineffective narrative structure."*

That paragraph is accurate, yes, but not nearly as likely to grab the audience's attention as this lesson's first sentence. In journalism parlance, the longer version "buried the lead" since it didn't start with the most important point.

Of everything we teach in our media training workshops, this may be the toughest lesson for spokespersons to incorporate into their answers. That's because most people have been taught to form logical arguments that build to rousing conclusions. And in some arenas, building a chronological argument *is* a useful method of communicating. For example, virtually every television legal drama features prosecuting attorneys delivering a climactic—and chronological—closing argument.

But for at least two reasons, the "beginning, middle, and end" approach to answering questions is ineffective for most forms of media interviewing:

1. **If you don't get it out fast, you might not get it out at all:** Beginning each answer with the most important point is especially important in live interviews, since most interviewers prefer fast-moving, dynamic segments. If you speak for too long, they may interrupt to ask a follow-up question before you ever get a chance to state your conclusion.

2. **It doesn't grab 'em by the throat:** You probably own a few books that you cast aside before you ever made it past page 20. That's because the author failed to grab your attention early, leading you to give up and find something better to do.

   Media spokespersons who start too slowly run the same risk but can avoid it by delivering their most compelling conclusions first. As the old advice teaches: "Grab 'em by the throat and don't let go."

Start most of your answers with your lead. Then if you have time, add context by going back to the beginning and middle, ending your answer by restating the lead. Here's an example:

Question: "What do you think of this new Social Security bill?"

Bad Answer: "Well, we've been advocating for an increase in Social Security payments for years, and this bill wouldn't do much to help. One of the reasons we're concerned about it is…"

Good Answer: "It's a terrible bill that will be devastating for senior citizens. That's because…"

The "bad" answer begins with background information and tepid language. The "good" one begins with a short, powerful conclusion, and continues by offering additional background.

WHY + WHAT

In the last lesson, you learned to begin most of your answers with the lead. But there's one time you should use a slightly *less direct* lead: when you're asked a broad question about your work, such as, "Can you tell me about your company?"

Ninety-nine times out of a hundred, spokespersons answer that type of open-ended question with a direct lead by saying something like:

> *"Well, the Association for the Advancement of Arkansas Education is a 501(c)3 nonprofit organization with 25 employees working in four statewide offices to improve elementary and secondary education in Arkansas."*

> *OR*

> *"Smith Toys is one of the leading companies in the United States making high-quality children's toys in an affordable and sustainable manner."*

I'm guessing neither of those statements grabbed you. They're not *bad*, since both conveyed real information, but they're rather bland and uninspiring.

Worse, neither statement is particularly original. It's easy to imagine that dozens of American companies manufacturing environmentally friendly toys could have answered the question in exactly the same way.

Those responses failed to get your attention because they answered a "what" question with a "what" answer.

Imagine if the spokespersons had answered the questions just a little differently, beginning with some context that explained *why* their work mattered. Their answers might have sounded more like these:

> *"Here in Arkansas, we rank 50th in the United States in high school graduation rates. That means our students are among*

*the least prepared in the nation when entering the workforce
and the most likely to live in poverty for the rest of their lives.
The Association for the Advancement of Arkansas Education
is dedicated to changing that and to making sure our students
get the high-quality education they need to successfully
compete in the global marketplace."*

OR

*"You know how children's toys always seem to cost too much
and break within weeks of opening the box? Well, Smith Toys
makes toys that are going to work for years after you open
the package—we guarantee it—and we've even figured out a
way to make high-quality toys that are both affordable and
environmentally friendly."*

I'm guessing those versions grabbed your attention more than the first ones. That's because both spokespersons formatted their responses as a "why + what" instead of just a "what."

You can use the "why + what" format every time you're asked an open-ended question such as:

- What does your company do?

- What is your organization's focus?

- Can you tell me about your product?

By themselves, "whats" just don't work very well. Most people don't care if you're a 501(c)3 charity, how many offices you have in the state, or whether you're a "leading" toy company. Those "whats" aren't going to initiate a rush of support to your brand.

So when you're asked an open-ended question, don't just tell them *what* your company does. Tell them *why* it matters.

31 SPEAK IN COMPLETE SENTENCES, UNLESS...

In almost all print interviews and many taped broadcast interviews, the audience will never hear the reporter's questions, only your answers. Therefore, you should begin each answer with a complete sentence that includes the question.

For example, if a reporter asks, "How many people are affected by this change in Medicare policy?" don't say, "Twenty million." The journalist is unlikely to quote you merely citing a statistic since that number doesn't make sense without context or further explanation.

Instead say, "This change to Medicare policy will affect 20 million people and will be absolutely devastating for millions of low-income seniors who will no longer be able to afford all of their medications." That response not only answers the direct question but also advances a clear message.

If you forget to answer a question in a complete sentence, some reporters will remind you to do so. It's okay to comply—as long as the reporter's question uses positive or neutral language. There's one critical caveat, though: if a question contains loaded language, don't repeat it back in your answer!

When you're asked a negative question such as, "Has your organization ever broken the law?" don't respond with, "Our organization has never broken the law." That "denial" quote will inevitably be the one the reporter uses, which will do you no favors in the court of public opinion. Why connect illegal activity and your organization in the same sentence?

Instead, frame your answer in positive terms: "We have always complied with the law." Then transition to one of your messages or message supports. That response gives reporters the complete sentence they need but doesn't repeat back the negative language that could haunt you when the story comes out.

THREE CASE STUDIES:
MEMORABLE NEGATIVE LANGUAGE (V)

Richard Nixon, 1973: "I'm not a crook."

In 1972, five men were arrested for breaking into the Democratic National Committee headquarters at the Watergate office building in Washington, DC. They were connected to President Richard Nixon, a Republican, who denied knowledge of the break-in.

In 1973, during the height of the Watergate scandal and nine months before his resignation, Mr. Nixon stood before a group of 400 reporters from the Associated Press. He boldly asserted, "I'm not a crook." Those words only made him look guiltier in the eyes of the public and became the most famous words he ever uttered.

Bill Clinton, 1998: "I did not have sexual relations with that woman."

Days after news broke in 1998 of a sexual affair between Democratic President Bill Clinton and White House intern Monica Lewinsky, the president stood in front of a bank of cameras, angrily wagged his finger, and denied that he had engaged in an inappropriate relationship.

Mr. Clinton stood by his denial for seven months until finally admitting that he had, in fact, had sexual relations with Ms. Lewinsky. His denial remains one of the most famous sound bites of his presidency.

Christine O'Donnell, 2010: "I'm not a witch."

Christine O'Donnell, Delaware's Republican candidate for the U.S. Senate, had to do damage control after a tape emerged of her saying a decade earlier that she had "dabbled into witchcraft." She took on her critics by releasing an ad that began with the words "I'm not a witch." The ad backfired and she became fodder for the late-night comics. She lost the race.

32 HOW TO BE A BETTER MEDIA GUEST IN THREE SECONDS

I know the title of this lesson sounds like a catchy headline offering impossible results. But I swear it's true—you *can* become a better media spokesperson in just three seconds.

Here's how:

1. When a reporter asks you a question, don't answer right away.

2. Remain quiet for a few seconds.

3. Think about your response.

4. Answer the question, but only when you're ready.

5. Repeat after each question.

That may sound like trite advice. But learning to pause is often the single most impactful thing a spokesperson can do.

Remaining quiet isn't easy. We're conditioned to respond immediately when someone asks us a question in everyday conversation, so it's little surprise that most of us instinctually respond the moment we're asked a question. In fact, that impulse is *so* powerful, our trainees often forget our advice to pause within seconds of hearing it. The moment the camera's red "record" light appears, their adrenaline surges—and their pauses are nowhere to be found.

But responding immediately prevents spokespersons from thinking through their answer before delivering it, which often leads to an inferior response; they'll speak aloud for a few seconds before finally stumbling onto their point. When spokespersons pause for a few seconds, their answers almost always become sharper, more focused, and devoid of the "uhhhs" that otherwise plague their replies.

You can almost always use this technique for print interviews. You can also insert pauses for many taped radio or television interviews, if the reporter only plans to air a few of your quotes, not the entire interview. Just do the editor a favor: if you look away while thinking during a taped television interview, look back up and wait a second before beginning your answer.

There are two critical times to ignore this lesson: during hostile interviews, when journalists may use your lengthy silences as an indication of your guilt, and during live interviews, when pauses can communicate evasiveness, a lack of confidence, or a lack of credibility.

If your interview is hostile or live (or both), you can still use this technique, at least in part. Although you can't pause for several seconds, you *can* allow the reporter to completely finish the question before rushing to speak. Too many people are unable to resist the temptation of jumping in before the question is completely asked, wasting a free pass to think for an extra couple of moments. That's especially important during hostile interviews, when a momentary pause allows you to slow the pace of the interview.

Practice this technique while answering questions in business meetings and speeches. You'll be shocked by how easy it is to become a better spokesperson in just three seconds.

SECTION FOUR

Answering The Tough Questions

"The questions don't do the damage. Only the answers do."

Sam Donaldson, ABC News

33 INTRODUCING THE ATMs

When we conduct challenging practice interviews with our clients, they occasionally fail to deliver a single message in any of their responses. When I ask them afterward what went wrong, they say, "You didn't ask me the right questions!"

You will rarely hear the "right" question. If you wait for a reporter to lob a big, juicy softball, you're going to be waiting a long time. Your job as a spokesperson is to get your messages out, even if the questions are off topic or hostile. To help you answer **difficult questions** with (relative) ease while remaining on message, I have developed a systematic method called the *ATMs*.

> ### ANSWERING TOUGH QUESTIONS
> ### IS AS EASY AS THE ATMs:
>
> **Answer**
>
> **Transition**
>
> **Message**
>
> **sell**

"A" stands for answering the question. You should answer every question, every time—if you don't, you risk appearing evasive. But as the phrase often attributed to Hippocrates advises, "First, do no harm." You can often answer off-topic questions in a single word or phrase. Examples of short answers include "Yes," "No," "Maybe," "Perhaps," "That's unclear," "That's not quite right," "Absolutely," and "Absolutely not."

"T" stands for transitioning, during which you'll use short phrases to help you get from *their* questions to *your* answers. The next lesson will go into more detail on this topic.

"M" stands for your messages and message supports.

Finally, **"s"** stands for selling your message by inserting a closing call to action. You might ask people to buy your product, visit your website, or support a new piece of legislation. The "s" is in lowercase because calls to action should only be used in *some* of your answers.

EXAMPLE: ANSWERING QUESTIONS WITH THE ATMs

QUESTION: "Why should your museum get more money from taxpayers? Times are tough for everyone. Shouldn't you have to sacrifice like everybody else?"

ANSWER: "Absolutely, and we have."

TRANSITION: "It's important to remember that…"

MESSAGE: "…we are only asking for enough money to keep our doors open and our artwork safe. A small increase would allow us to remain open during hours that are convenient for families to visit so they can enjoy the amazing works that few cities of our size have."

sell: "That's why we're asking the public to contact the governor's office and request the funding we need."

Aim to spend just 10—20 percent of your answer in the "A" and "T" (the *getting-to*-the-message parts) and 80—90 percent of your answer in the "M" and "s" (the *actual* message parts).

You can use the ATMs several times in an interview, but avoid using it for every answer, which can appear inauthentic.

Finally, always bear in mind that tough questions can be terrific opportunities to demonstrate your competence. Instead of fearing tough questions, remember that you can enhance your credibility with the audience by answering them well.

Note: Your transition may occasionally be able to serve as your "A" <u>and</u> *your "T." In those cases, drop the "A" and skip directly to the "T."*

34 TRANSITIONING

If a reporter asks you a straightforward question, just answer it—you don't need a transition phrase for the easy ones. But when reporters ask an off-topic or "trick" question, it's your job to steer the interview back to your messages or message supports. Transition phrases are intended to help you do that.

After you answer the reporter's question (often in a single word or phrase), you can use one of these transition phrases—or one of your own—to serve as a bridge between their question and your messages:

- "It's important to remember that…"

- "Keep in mind that…"

- "Here's what we've been hearing from our members…"

- "Let me tell you what we've been seeing…"

- "I'm not sure that's the case…"

- "However…"

- "Here's what we know…"

- "But even more importantly…"

- "That said, what we see as an even bigger issue is…"

- "The main thing we're focusing on is…"

- "What our research shows is…"

As for what to transition *to*, listen carefully to the reporter's question and transition to the message or message support that most closely relates to it.

Transition lines are also helpful for two other reasons:

1. **They Act as Verbal Flags:** Imagine you're listening to the radio when the guest suddenly says, "Yes, but the most important thing to remember is…" You're unlikely to flip to a different station at that moment, since you'd want to know what the most important thing is. That type of verbal flagging focuses the audience's attention and helps people remember your most important points.

2. **They Prevent Brain Freezes:** If you're on the air and suddenly go blank, you can use a transition line followed by one of your messages. That may sound awkward to the audience, but it's a whole lot better than blushing and saying, "Sorry, I forgot what I was saying."

PRESIDENT OBAMA USES THE ATMs (V)

During a press conference in November 2010, Mr. Obama used a transition phrase to answer a question about the economy.

QUESTION: "The idea that your policies are taking the country in reverse—you just reject that idea altogether that your policies could be going in reverse?"

ANSWER: "Yes. And I think, look, here's the bottom line. When I came into office, this economy was in freefall, and the economy has stabilized. The economy is growing. We've seen nine months of private-sector job growth."

Here's a breakdown of his reply:

ANSWER: "Yes."

TRANSITION: "And I think, look, here's the bottom line."

MESSAGE: The rest of his answer, which highlighted his administration's economic achievements.

sell: There was no "s" in that answer. If he had wanted to use one, he might have added, "That's why I'm asking the American people to contact their members of Congress and tell them to support our new jobs program."

35 THE SEVEN-SECOND STRAY

In the late 1990s, I was a producer for CNN's Sunday public-affairs program, *Late Edition with Wolf Blitzer*. Because *Late Edition* aired after all of the other Sunday public-affairs shows, one of my tasks each week was to watch the earlier programs to monitor what politicians were saying. If a politician said something interesting, I'd edit a video clip out of the quote so that Wolf could air it on the show.

I was always on the lookout for a politician saying something off message. Why? Because anything unscripted and off-the-cuff was inherently more interesting than the canned responses we always heard. And in a newsroom, a less scripted response will almost always be deemed more newsworthy.

Years later, I developed a name to describe that phenomenon: "the seven-second stray." I call it that because if a spokesperson is on message for 59 minutes 53 seconds of an hour-long interview but says something off message for just seven seconds, I can virtually guarantee that the reporter will select that seven-second answer to play over and over again.

The seven-second stray can be deadly. Not only is it often damaging to your reputation, but it drowns out everything else you've said, becoming the only quote the audience will remember from your interview.

My choice of the word *drown* in the previous sentence is intentional. To help our clients avoid committing a seven-second stray, I often use the analogy of a lifeboat. If you're facing tough questioning, I tell them, your message is your lifeboat. If you keep returning to your message and message supports—stories, statistics, and sound bites—it's as if you're swimming to the safety of the closest lifeboat. But if you stray off message, you're treading water at best—if not drifting farther and farther away from the lifeboat until that inevitable (and entirely predictable) moment when you drown.

CASE STUDY:
BP CEO'S INFAMOUS SEVEN-SECOND STRAY (V)

In April 2010, an oil rig exploded in the Gulf of Mexico, killing 11 men and injuring 17 others. For 87 days, oil gushed from the seafloor, washing up on ecologically sensitive shorelines from Texas to Florida. The spill wrecked local economies, leaving tens of thousands of people out of work. Fishermen were left without seafood to sell, hotels were left without guests, and restaurants were left without diners.

British Petroleum, the massive oil conglomerate responsible for the rig, took a daily beating in the press. The bad press had a devastating impact on the company: the oil giant quickly shed half of its worth, a loss of more than $100 billion.

As bad as the crisis was, the spill itself wasn't responsible for the greatest harm to BP's reputation. Rather, the company's inept response, headed by CEO Tony Hayward, significantly deepened the damage. In a televised interview, Mr. Hayward famously quipped:

> *"There's no one who wants this thing over more than I do. You know, I'd like my life back."*

That stunningly tone-deaf seven-second stray, which slighted the deceased oil workers and newly unemployed workers, became a symbol of BP's self-interested focus. Those five telling words, "I'd like my life back," reinforced an irreversible narrative of a clueless company that just didn't get it – and just didn't care.

Mr. Hayward was forced out shortly after the spill ended, but it didn't matter. The damage to BP had already been done.

36 THREE DANGEROUS TYPES OF REPORTERS

Most reporters aren't out to get you. But since there are always a few who will try to get you to say something you'll later regret, this lesson will help you survive your interactions with three of the most dangerous types of reporters.

DANGEROUS TYPE 1: THE FRIENDLY GUY AT THE BAR

One night when I was out to dinner with a female friend, she looked over to the bar and groaned. She told me that a man had just started hitting on a woman sitting alone, but in the sleazy way that makes women cringe. She said that all women know "that guy."

He's the man at the bar who approaches a female stranger and begins to chat her up. He thinks he's being slick, but the woman can instinctively sense his ulterior motives. Still, he persists.

He agrees a little too easily with everything she says and laughs a little too loudly at her jokes. He's waiting for that moment when (he hopes) she will agree to go home with him.

Some reporters have something in common with that guy: They'll say what they have to say to get what they want. Sometimes, that means they'll try to coax something out of you that you'll later regret saying.

The "friendly" reporter aims to make you feel comfortable so that you begin speaking freely. But when the story runs, you're devastated to find that he abused your trust by printing some of your most damning statements. But he didn't abuse your trust. His loyalty was always to the story, not to you.

Never confuse the genuine kindness of a reporter for that of a friend's. Be friendly, be warm, be outgoing—but never disclose things you might later regret.

DANGEROUS TYPE 2: THE QUIET TYPE

Have you ever been in a conversation with someone who just keeps staring at you once you've finished speaking? If you're like most people, you feel awkward and quickly start talking again to fill the uncomfortable silence.

Reporters bank on that awkward dynamic and know you'll say the most damaging things after you've finished your "official" answer. Instead of falling into this trap, just remain quiet after completing your answer, or say something such as, "That's the main point. What other questions can I answer for you?"

DANGEROUS TYPE 3: THE JERK

I once had to deal with a very nasty reporter from a national news organization on behalf of one of our clients. He relished asking aggressive questions in the most hostile manner possible, and I found it tough not to react defensively. I finally learned to ignore his tone and rewrite his question in my mind, a good technique if you find yourself in a similar situation.

For example, if he asked:

> *"Your group hasn't accomplished anything. When will you stop wasting people's money and give up already?"*

I would rewrite his question in my mind to something less hostile, such as:

> *"Can you tell me about your accomplishments?*

Then I would calmly respond:

> *"I disagree with your question's premise, and am happy
> to share a few of our accomplishments with you. First, we
> recently..."*

37 STAY COOL, BABY!

In order to assess the skill level of each of our trainees, we often conduct an on-camera "baseline" interview at the beginning of each media training session.

It's amazing to watch our trainees' reactions just before we begin. They're usually visibly nervous, wondering, What is this guy going to ask me? Do I have good answers to his questions? Can I get through this without saying anything stupid?

They don't actually *say* those things. But I can see those thoughts etched on their faces and sense them through their defensive body language. They may as well just cross their arms over their faces, lean back, and cower—their bodies are emitting that same message anyway.

That defensiveness is a major problem, and it can undermine even the most perfect message. Defensiveness—in the form of closed gestures, a tight smile, or abruptly clipped answers—leads the audience to wonder what you're hiding.

In order to help our trainees, I encourage them to change their interior monologues before they begin their second round of practice interviews. Instead of, "Oh, no, here come the tough questions," I ask them to try, "I'm so happy you asked me that, because your question gives me an opportunity to discuss that issue." You'd be amazed by how much that small mental adjustment helps them convey a more open tone. That openness not only helps to persuade the audience but also defangs most interviewers, who are less inclined to probe a spokesperson who appears to have little to hide.

Beyond the fear of the unexpected question, defensiveness comes across in at least three other ways, which a surprising number of spokespersons exhibit on a regular basis:

1. **Anger:** As questions become tougher, it becomes even more critical for you to maintain open and non-defensive body language (more on body language in section five). Audiences award points to spokespersons who exhibit grace under pressure and deduct them from people who offer heated responses.

   Anger also undermines an automatic dynamic that works in your favor. Ted Koppel, my former boss and the long-time host of ABC's *Nightline*, says that an audience's allegiance is to the interviewer, not to the person being interviewed—at least at the beginning. But if viewers perceive that the interviewer is being unfair, the audience will shift its sympathy from the journalist to the interviewee. So stay cool, and the audience may automatically move your way.

2. **Sarcasm:** In everyday life, you may occasionally win an argument by making a well-timed sarcastic point. But media interviews aren't debates, and you don't always win points for your rapier wit. On the contrary, sarcasm can make you appear peevish and unlikeable. Remember that in many formats, the public will never see the question you were asked, only your answer. So even if your sarcastic reply looks fine "in context," it won't look good as a stand-alone sound bite.

3. **Walking Away:** My blog regularly documents instances when spokespersons abruptly end an interview and walk off the set. I've yet to see one that makes the spokesperson look good. Unless the reporter has become downright abusive, don't walk off—the moment you do, you lose. Walk-offs make for dramatic television and help stations attract viewers—so you better believe that the video of your humiliating walk-off will be played repeatedly, and could live forever on the Internet.

38 THEY'LL BEAT YOU WITH A STICK

My favorite media-interviewing story of all time comes from someone I met years ago at a conference, an education expert named Clint.

Clint was no media novice. He was an experienced media guest who consistently delighted journalists with his obvious expertise and charismatic delivery. He prepared for media interviews carefully, crafting his messages and knowing the precise points he wanted to get across.

One day, he sat down for an interview with John Stossel. Mr. Stossel was the co-anchor of ABC's *20/20* at the time, on which he had earned a reputation for confronting guests in rather dramatic fashion. The interview began smoothly enough. Stossel asked his questions, and Clint responded with his usual ease.

But things suddenly went awry. Stossel suddenly belted, "STOP TAPE!" Bolting to his feet, he turned to one of Clint's associates and screamed, "Is he *always* this boring?!?"

For the next three minutes, Stossel threw a temper tantrum. As his face turned plum red, he finally turned and gave Clint an ultimatum: "If you don't tell us who's getting screwed here, this entire interview is useless."

Clint was thrown. He was decidedly out of his element—and the combination of hot lights, giant studio cameras, and a famous but suddenly out-of-control anchorman was intimidating. Even though he was an experienced media guest, he'd never seen anything quite like that. So Clint decided to comply with Stossel's request.

Stossel returned to his seat, instructed the cameraman to roll tape, and heatedly asked: "So who's getting screwed here?"

"I'll tell you who's getting screwed here," Clint said, his finger wagging dramatically. "The American taxpayer, that's who!" In the shadows of the TV studio, Clint's associate buried his face in his hands. After the interview, the associate begged Stossel's producers not to run that clip. Not only did they ignore his pleas, they ran the incendiary clip at the top of the show:

> *Announcer: "Tonight, on 20/20"*
>
> *Clint: "I'll tell you who's getting screwed here—the American taxpayer, that's who!"*

Mr. Stossel got what he wanted—a dramatic and television-friendly sound bite. But I doubt he was ever *actually* upset. He likely used a dramatic technique to knock his guest off message and elicit a more unscripted reply. And although it made for good TV, it wasn't the sound bite Clint wanted.

What should Clint have done? He could have simply said:

> *"Mr. Stossel, I'm sorry you think my answers aren't heartfelt. I believe passionately in every word I'm telling you. I'd be happy to continue the interview with you, but I have to do it in a manner that represents who I truly am."*

Reporters may use a dramatic technique to throw you off stride, like Mr. Stossel did, or they might ask the same question in eight different ways until you finally lose your patience and offer a snippy reply.

Your job is the same regardless of the provocation: to answer in a controlled manner. In edited interviews, the public will never see the reporter baiting you, and they won't hear the reporter asking you the same question eight different times. They'll only see the one answer you delivered in an annoyed tone. So keep your audience in mind, and don't take the bait.

39 THE AMBUSH INTERVIEW

When most people think of ambush interviews, they think of a television interviewer chasing after a scandal-tarred executive with camera and microphone in tow.

Those types of ambushes *do* occur occasionally, but they're rare. More typically, an ambush occurs in one of two ways:

1. When a reporter shows up without notice.

2. When a reporter deviates from the agreed-upon topic to blindside a source with something totally unexpected.

In both cases, the reporter is after one thing: a great visual that makes you look guilty. If you respond with defensiveness, anger, or shock, the news outlet will run the tape of your bad reaction repeatedly, perhaps for days.

You win an ambush by denying the reporter a great visual. If you're ever ambushed, remember the advice offered in that old deodorant ad: never let 'em see you sweat. By remaining calm, you prevent reporters from getting the compelling "money shot" they desire.

CASE STUDY: PRESIDENT REAGAN: "WHAT? I CAN'T HEAR YOU."

President Reagan, a master of good visuals, was subject to an ambush of sorts every time he exited the White House to board *Marine One*.

Sam Donaldson, ABC News' aggressive White House Correspondent, would shout tough questions at him as he walked across the lawn.

As the blades of the helicopter whirred, Reagan pretended he couldn't hear Donaldson's questions by cupping a hand to his ear, shrugging, and offering a mile-wide smile.

1. WHEN A REPORTER SHOWS UP WITHOUT NOTICE

What should you say when a reporter shows up without warning? Try something like this:

> *"Thank you for coming. I'd be happy to speak with you. I wish I knew you were coming—I have a meeting scheduled that I'm already running late for. Please contact my office so we can set up a time to talk."*

Then walk to your destination. If you only have a short distance to walk, continue facing the reporter and restate your message as you walk backward to avoid the "back to camera" shot. And whatever you do, don't block the camera by placing your hand over the lens! Deny them the defensive-looking visual.

2. WHEN A REPORTER BLINDSIDES YOU DURING AN INTERVIEW

What do you do when you've agreed to an interview about your organization's work to save endangered tigers but the reporter suddenly asks about your lavish compensation package? If you refuse to answer, you look guilty. If you answer badly, the results could be even worse.

You have two choices:

1. **Answer the question.** Doing so usually plays better to the audience, and good media training should prepare you in advance to anticipate the "unexpected" questions.

2. **Deflect the question.** Tell the reporter that this interview was supposed to be about your work to save tigers, but that you'd be happy to schedule a future interview to discuss other issues. This might be your best option if the question is about a topic the audience wouldn't expect you to know much about, and may be your best approach if answering the question badly would do even more harm than not answering it at all.

40 ANSWERING QUESTIONS WHEN YOU DON'T KNOW THE ANSWERS

The next few lessons will address 10 types of questions reporters often ask, all of which can be tricky for spokespersons.

The first of those questions terrifies many spokespersons most: the question to which they don't know the answer. The good news is that their terror is usually unnecessary. That's because the tricky part lies less in the question than in your answer. But if you deliver a factually incorrect response during a challenging interview, you can be sure it will be used against you in the news story—so never offer an answer unless you know it's true. If you're stumped during an interview, you have two choices:

OPTION 1: "I DON'T KNOW"

You can simply say "I don't know." If the question is about something you should know or can get an answer to, tell the reporter you'll follow up with a more complete reply.

But as the last lesson explained, an "I don't know" answer can make you look bad on topics you're expected to know something about. In those cases and others, consider using the second option instead.

OPTION 2: "THE PETER JENNINGS RULE"

When I'm stumped during an interview, I'm fond of using something I've dubbed "The Peter Jennings Rule."

A former ABC News colleague told me that Peter Jennings, the late anchor of ABC's *World News Tonight,* used to test his correspondents by asking them a question on live television to which they might not know the answer. His correspondents learned to answer the question by saying something such as:

> *"Well, that's unclear, Peter, but here's what we know at this hour…"*

The skill is to tell the public what you know, not what you don't. Imagine you're a physician and a morning show host asks you how many people die from lung cancer in the United States every year. Instead of saying "I don't know" or fumbling to find the right statistic, you might say:

> *"Thousands of people still die from lung cancer in the U.S. every year, but the good news is that the number is going down. As people continue to quit smoking and fewer people pick up the habit, I expect the numbers to continue dropping."*

Instead of providing the audience with no value whatsoever by saying you didn't know, you told them something about lung cancer rates that you *did* know. Many interviewers won't press you for the specific number after you provide an answer of value. If they do, *then* it's okay to say you don't know.

There are moments when it's embarrassing if you don't know something you should. For example, many political candidates are made to look out of touch when they can't recall the current minimum wage. Instead of simply saying "I don't know," imagine if they said:

> *"Here's what I know. It's too low, and we need to make sure America's working class continues to thrive. My priority is to create good middle-class jobs that pay a real living wage."*

That may not be poetry, but it does succeed in avoiding the type of media gaffe that cable news stations love to air dozens of times each day.

Finally, if you're not the right person to answer a given question, it's okay to say so. It's rarely a bad idea for specialists to "stay in their lanes" and refer off-topic questions to other specialists. So if you're a company financial officer and you're asked about a manufacturing process, just tell the reporter that you're not an expert on that topic but would be happy to find someone who is.

41 ANSWERING QUESTIONS THAT CALL FOR SPECULATION

Reporters frequently ask media spokespersons to gaze into their crystal balls and tell them what the future looks like.

Some of those "speculation" questions are innocuous: if you're a software designer and you're asked what changes you think will emerge in the industry over the next five years, it's okay to provide your analysis of where you think things are headed.

But many speculation questions are dangerous. Your answers can make a situation appear worse than it really is—and if you guess badly, your wrong answers can damage your credibility.

For example, imagine that the director of a nonprofit group lobbying for better safety regulations of toxic household cleansers is asked whether the state legislature is going to pass the bill she supports this year. If she answers "yes," she'd better be right. That's because the media will inevitably ask her about her incorrect prediction if the bill doesn't pass, and her wrong answer might diminish her credibility with the public and the press for future stories.

Instead, she can use a variation of the ATMs to answer this question:

> *(A) I'm reluctant to speculate, (T) but I can tell you that (M) the majority of lawmakers I've spoken to have told me that they recognize how important this bill is to protect children from dangerous household cleansers and that they plan to vote for it. (s) We still need as much support as possible, though, so I'd ask everybody watching this to call their representative and tell them to vote 'yes.'"*

As illustrated by the example above, it's usually best to deflect questions that call for speculation by saying something along the lines of, "I can't speculate, but here's what I can tell you..."

CASE STUDY: TREASURY SECRETARY
SPECULATES INCORRECTLY

In an April 2011 interview, U.S. Treasury Secretary Timothy Geithner appeared on the Fox Business Network to discuss the possibility of the U.S. credit rating being downgraded:

> *Peter Barnes (Host): "Is there a risk that the United States could lose its triple-A credit rating, yes or no?"*
>
> *Geithner: "No risk of that. No risk."*
>
> *Barnes: "So Standard and Poor's is wrong, the United States will keep its triple-A credit rating?"*
>
> *Geithner: "Absolutely."*

Four months later, rating agency Standard and Poor's downgraded the U.S. credit rating for the first time in the nation's history. Cable news channels played the video clip of Mr. Geithner's overly confident (and incorrect) answer for days, and political opponents pointed to that moment as evidence that he should resign his post.

Mr. Geithner could have answered the question by saying something like this:

> *"Let me tell you what we're doing to make sure we retain our triple-A rating..."*

Apply the same technique for hypothetical questions. Your job is to share what you know, not to answer "what if" questions. It might be appropriate to answer a hypothetical question about a *specific* situation with a *general* answer about how you would approach your decision making in that case. But that approach often leads to even more questions intended to get you to be more specific (plus, your *general* answers might be applied to the *specific* situation), so be cautious and practice in advance.

42 ANSWERING QUESTIONS THAT SEEK YOUR PERSONAL OPINION

Imagine that you're the spokesperson for a government agency and your division just passed a new regulation to enhance the testing of imported beef.

Despite the department's enthusiasm for the new rules, you don't personally believe the new regulations will keep beef safer. In fact, you're convinced the rules were passed primarily to satisfy safety advocates—not to protect consumers—and you're pretty sure the move will ultimately cost diners more money for no good reason.

So when a reporter asks whether you personally believe the regulations will help, you have a dilemma: Should you say what you really think or represent the views of the agency?

These conflicts between personal opinion and company policy occur frequently, and I regularly see them play out in our media training workshops.

The correct answer is almost always to speak on behalf of your company, organization, or agency. There are exceptions, of course: if you have a strong moral objection to the view you're being asked to espouse, you're probably not the right spokesperson for that topic. But it's usually better to handle those disputes internally rather than airing them in the press. Otherwise, it's probably time to seek new work.

Some spokespersons wonder whether they can express a personal opinion so long as they tell the reporter:

> *"This is my personal opinion, not the view of the company."*

No way. The reporter will still identify you as a representative of the company, and your conflicting view will undercut the view you're being paid to articulate.

Instead, tell the reporter that you're speaking as a representative of the company and that it would be inappropriate for personal views to enter into the conversation.

You can use the ATMs to answer personal opinion questions, as in the following exchange:

> Question: "What do you think personally? Will these new regulations governing imported beef help make food safer?"
>
> Answer: "(A) I'm speaking on behalf of the agency (T) and can tell you what we believe. (M) We're confident that these new regulations will keep Americans safer. Here's how…"

CASE STUDY: WHOLE FOODS CHAIRMAN'S "PERSONAL" OPINION

In 2009, John Mackey, chairman of Whole Foods, sparked an uprising from his largely progressive customer base when he wrote an op-ed for *The Wall Street Journal* opposing President Obama's health care reform proposal.

After customers began boycotting his stores, he defended himself by writing, "I was asked to write an op-ed piece and I gave my personal opinions…Whole Foods as a company has no official position on the issue."

His defense didn't work. Many customers continued to boycott his stores. Within a few months, Mr. Mackey stepped down as chairman (though he retained the title of CEO).

Personal opinions are occasionally appropriate in a personal profile piece, the very purpose of which is to get to know someone better. But spokespersons should be careful not to say anything that contradicts their organization's views, or reporters will seize on and highlight those differences in the final news story (more on personal profiles in lesson 68).

43 ANSWERING A PARAPHRASED QUESTION

Many years ago, I led the media shop at Conservation International (CI), one of the world's largest environmental nonprofit groups.

We landed a big media appearance when ABC's *Nightline* agreed to air a half-hour broadcast on CI's plan to protect vulnerable species. ABC sent reporter Robert Krulwich—a journalist with a rather flamboyant style—to interview CI's president, Russ Mittermeier.

Conservation International President Russ
Mittermeier with a furry friend.

At the time, CI's diverse board of directors included everyone from actor Harrison Ford and Intel co-founder Gordon Moore to Jordan's Queen Noor and a Mexican concrete company executive.

Mr. Krulwich clearly had a plan in mind—he thought the board was "radical," and he wanted Mr. Mittermeier to say so. As Krulwich pressed on with his questioning, I got increasingly nervous that he'd get what he wanted.

It's been several years, but the exchange went something like this:

Krulwich: "Your board is somewhat radical, yes?"

Mittermeier: "I wouldn't say that. I'd say they're passionate, engaged, and forward thinking."

Krulwich: "But if you define radical as passionate, engaged, and forward thinking, they're pretty radical, right?"

Mittermeier: "I wouldn't use that word."

Mr. Krulwich's paraphrasing was a clever attempt to put words in Mittermeier's mouth, and I suspect the majority of spokespersons would have fallen for it. But Mittermeier was a seasoned spokesperson who refused to let Krulwich get the quote he wanted.

Better yet, Mittermeier didn't even utter the word "radical," denying Krulwich a potential sound bite.

If a reporter paraphrases your words, don't accept the paraphrase unless it's completely accurate. If it's not, correct the statement in your own words without using any of the reporter's loaded language.

> *If a reporter paraphrases your words, don't accept the paraphrase unless it's completely accurate. If it's not, correct the statement in your own words without using any of the reporter's loaded language.*

Why did it matter to Mittermeier? Because a headline with the phrase "Radical Environmental Group" wouldn't have helped promote CI's brand, which was that of a pragmatic environmental group open to partnering with industry. It would have reinforced stereotypes about "radical environmentalism" that wouldn't have been accurate in CI's case.

44 ANSWERING QUESTIONS THAT PRESENT FALSE CHOICES

If you had to choose, which would you say you care more about: your child's health or your child's happiness?

Just *try* answering that question without sounding bad. If you answer "health," you'll be asked why a healthy but miserable child is acceptable to you. If you answer "happiness," one might inquire why you'd be satisfied with a happy but sickly kid.

Reporters love questions that present false choices, since your answers will inevitably make their stories more exciting. But they're bad for you as a spokesperson, so be wary of them.

There are many types of false choice questions, but they usually fall into one of two categories: "this or that" and "yes or no."

1. THIS ONE OR THAT ONE?

The question at the top of this page is a classic "this one or that one" question, intended to force you to select from two unappealing, black-and-white options. But just because a reporter phrases a question as a choice between "A" and "B" doesn't mean you have to play along in your response.

In the above example, you might respond by saying:

> *"Asking me to choose between my child's health and happiness is like being forced to choose between air and water. Both are critical to life, and I hope never to have to make such a choice."*

Politicians are often asked questions such as, "Is your top priority cutting the deficit or growing the economy?" The answer to that question is:

"Well, we have to do both. We can't cut the deficit without growing the economy, and we can't grow the economy without cutting the deficit. My plan addresses both. Here's how...."

2. YES OR NO?

Not all "yes or no" questions are intended as traps. In fact, the best way to retain your credibility is often to concede an obvious point by offering a direct "yes" or "no" reply. For example, you should feel free to answer a "yes or no" question directly if a reporter asks a question with an obvious answer: "Are you disappointed that the product you released last year sold fewer than half the units you predicted?"

Still, many other "yes or no" questions *are* insidious. That's because they have obvious answers and everyone watching the interview knows it—but there's no way for you to respond with a direct "yes" or "no" without the resulting quote being awful.

For example, let's say you're a spokesperson for a local hospital. You're asked, "Yes or no, do your patients ever complain about your hospital's nursing shortage?" You answer by saying:

"Yes, our patients occasionally tell us that they wish we had more nurses on duty, but most of our patients are very happy."

But as a result of saying "yes," the news story may read:

"Spokesman Bob Smith admitted that patients have been complaining about the hospital's lack of nurses."

If you think that answering a "yes or no" question may make you look bad, you can answer along these lines:

"Despite the nursing shortage in the region, our patients are overwhelmingly happy with the service they receive from our nurses. In fact, one survey found that our nursing staff has a higher satisfaction rate than any other hospital in the region."

45 ANSWERING QUESTIONS FROM LEFT FIELD

Your interview is going well when, all of a sudden, the reporter throws a completely unexpected question at you.

Those questions from "left field" are among the toughest to handle during a media interview. Some reporters may even intentionally set you up for the kill by asking easy questions early on to make you feel comfortable before catching you off guard with an entirely unanticipated question toward the end.

In lesson 39, you learned two ways to handle unexpected questions in an ambush: to answer the question or tell the reporter you'd happily schedule a follow-up interview regarding the unexpected topic. You can use those two techniques here as well.

But since not all left-field questions are "ambushes," this lesson will give you three additional techniques for coping with any unexpected questions:

1. **Pledge to learn more:** In many situations, particularly those in which the audience wouldn't expect you to know all of the facts, it's often best to pledge to learn more and get back to the reporter with a response. For example, let's say the reporter asks you about one of your senior managers, who was arrested for drunken driving over the weekend. If you haven't heard about the incident yet, tell the reporter you'd like an opportunity to look into it before responding.

2. **Talk about what you do know:** In lesson 40, you learned what to say when you don't know the answer. You can use the "Peter Jennings Rule" here as well, with an answer such as, "I don't know all of the specifics of the alleged incident you mentioned, but I can tell you that we take allegations of that sort very seriously…"

3. **Zoom out and generalize:** If the reporter's question is about a specific point, answer the question by zooming out and giving a more general response: "As a matter of policy, we don't speak about legal matters involving any of our employees, but I can tell you that whenever we learn of a potential incident, we immediately begin an internal investigation and take any necessary disciplinary actions promptly."

As you read in lesson 41, this approach can lead to more challenging follow-up questions, so practice in advance.

CASE STUDY: EXECUTIVE FACES TOUGH LEFT-FIELD QUESTION (V)

John Hirst, head of the British weather service, was caught completely off guard in 2010 when BBC host Andrew Neil opened an interview with this left-field question:

"You predicted a barbecue summer for 2009—we don't remember that—and a mild winter for this winter, which hasn't happened. Why did you receive a massive performance-related bonus?"

At first, Mr. Hirst deflected the salary question and praised his agency's accuracy. But the host undermined Mr. Hirst's claims for the next five minutes by citing one inaccurate forecast after another. Instead, Mr. Hirst could have "zoomed out" to give a response:

"The question isn't whether our forecasts are perfect, but whether they are among the most sophisticated and accurate in the world. They are. For every example you can cite of an incorrect forecast, I could cite many more that we got right. My bonus isn't tied to any specific forecast, but rather to our overall accuracy. You don't have to take my word for it—virtually every international meteorological group cites our office as among the best in the world."

46 ANSWERING QUESTIONS CONTAINING A FALSE PREMISE AND QUESTIONS SEEKING A GUARANTEE

QUESTIONS CONTAINING A FALSE PREMISE

When you were in grade school, you might have responded to a false accusation from a fellow student by saying something like, "I did not, you big fat liar!"

When reporters ask you a question that contains an incorrect premise, you should react the exact same way. (No, not by calling them a name, but by immediately rejecting the charge.) Failing to rebut a false premise gives more credence to the allegation, since the public will conclude that you would have corrected the record if the question contained an inaccuracy.

When answering a question containing a false premise, begin your response with one of these phrases (or something similar):

"I disagree with the premise of your question, because..."

"That's not accurate. What is accurate is that..."

"Actually, that's not quite right."

You can answer false-premise questions with the ATMs by omitting the "A" and using one of the above lines as your "T." For example:

> *Question: "Senator, you didn't invest a lot of money in building new infrastructure during your first term. If re-elected, will that be a bigger priority in your second term?*
>
> *Answer: "(T) I don't agree with the premise of your question. (M) I voted for two bills that increased spending for new roads and bridges in Minnesota by more than $150 million, and I will continue to support smart infrastructure projects that respect the taxpayers' money in my second term."*

QUESTIONS THAT DEMAND A GUARANTEE

There's one question that almost always trips up our trainees: the question that demands a guarantee. Like the "yes or no" question, a question demanding a guarantee is insidious, because everyone watching knows you can't guarantee anything in life with certainty. But if you answer by saying something flip such as, "There are no guarantees in life," or, "No, we can't guarantee that," the resulting quote will be dreadful.

The best way to answer "guarantee" questions is to talk about what you *can* guarantee. You usually can't guarantee a specific result, but you *can* guarantee that you are committed to something specific—an effort, a policy, or an idea.

Answer guarantee questions by dropping the "A" in the ATMs and using a phrase such as "Here's what I can guarantee" as your "T" before proceeding to your "M" and "s."

For example, let's say you're the director of a nonprofit organization that recently admitted to inappropriate use of some of the donations it received. A back and forth with a reporter might go:

> *Question: "More than $125,000 of the donations you received last year were used for expensive dinners and first-class travel, not for the programs you promised to apply them to. Can you guarantee your donors that not even a dime of their money will ever be misused again?"*

> *Answer: "(T) Here's what I can guarantee: (M) We will put into place every available safeguard to prevent this from ever happening again. For example, we're hiring an expert in fraud prevention to oversee our accounting department, and we are investing in the most sophisticated fraud-detection software on the market. Our donors expect their money to be used wisely, and so do I."*

47 ANSWERING QUESTIONS ABOUT YOUR COMPETITION AND QUESTIONS CONTAINING AN INDIRECT ATTRIBUTION

QUESTIONS ABOUT YOUR COMPETITION

By now, you know that reporters like to introduce conflict into a story, since pitting one side against another makes for rather dramatic copy. So if you say something negative about a competitor, it's a safe bet that your quote will end up in the final story, if not as the headline.

Still, there may be times when you *want* to say something critical about your competition. If you believe that your competitor's product is inferior to your own, for example, it's okay to say so—informing the public about *their* product's drawbacks might help increase *your* product's market share. Just make sure that your critical answer is part of a deliberate media strategy, not something you improvise during an interview.

QUESTIONS ABOUT COMPETITORS: USING THE ATMs

If you don't want to comment on your competitors, you can use the ATMs to help frame your answer, as follows:

QUESTION: *"Do you think your competitor's software has lived up to its potential?"*

If you say, "No, I don't," the headline may read, "Company X's Software a Flop, Says Company Y." If that's not the headline you want, you can use the ATMs as follows:

ANSWER: *"(A) I'll let Company X speak for itself, (T) but I can tell you why our software has been such a hit with consumers. (M) Our software has fewer glitches than any other product on the market, which has resulted in more repeat business than any other brand. In addition..."*

QUESTIONS WITH AN INDIRECT ATTRIBUTION

In a classic episode of *The West Wing*, Press Secretary C.J. Cregg (Allison Janney) warns the president's daughter, Zoey Bartlet (Elisabeth Moss), about the dangers of answering a question containing an indirect attribution:

> *C.J. Cregg to Zoey Bartlet: "Diane likes to keep things warm, casual, but she'll try to zing you with some indirect attribution like 'People say,' or 'There's a rumor that.'"*

Reporters who use such shaky attribution can ask virtually anything. If they can find two people willing to proffer a theory that you're an alien from outer space, they can ask, "People say you're a Martian. Can you respond?"

Unless the indirect attribution is about a topic that has become so pervasive that you *must* address it in order to move forward, don't discuss comments attributed to anonymous parties. Otherwise, the story will focus on your reaction to the comments rather than on your messages. Dismiss them quickly and move back to your message, as in these two examples:

> *"I'm not going to spend a lot of time addressing what an unnamed person might have said, but let me be absolutely clear about our priorities regarding that matter. They are...."*

> *"That's not correct. It's difficult to respond to anonymous parties without knowing their motives, but let me say that..."*

Occasionally, you may get a question with a *direct* attribution that you shouldn't comment on. For example, if a reporter asks you to comment on a study you've never seen before, you can say:

> *"I haven't seen the study you just cited and would like an opportunity to examine it before commenting on it."*

SECTION FIVE

Body Language
And Attire Guide

*"What you do speaks so loud that
I cannot hear what you say."*

Ralph Waldo Emerson, American writer

48 WHY BODY LANGUAGE MATTERS

Next time you travel to a new city, turn on the television in your hotel room. Mute the volume and flip the channels until you find a local station with a news anchor you've never seen before.

Almost immediately—without hearing a single word—you'll form an impression of the anchor. She seems smart, you might think, or beautiful, or bubbly. He looks like an artificial Ken doll, you might conclude, or kind, or obnoxious.

That automatic response might *seem* superficial—but it's actually quite human, and there's a good chance your gut reaction is right.

FROM *BLINK* BY MALCOLM GLADWELL

"The psychologist Nalini Ambady once gave [college] students three ten-second videotapes of a teacher—with the sound turned off—and found they had no difficulty at all coming up with a rating of the teacher's effectiveness. Then Ambady cut the clips back to five seconds, and the ratings were the same. They were remarkably consistent even when she showed students just *two* seconds of videotape. Then Ambady compared those snap judgments of teacher effectiveness with evaluations of those same professors after a full semester of classes, and she found they were also essentially the same."

That means the impression you leave with an audience may have little to do with your words. In fact, some communications studies suggest that in certain circumstances, your appearance and delivery have *more* impact than the words you choose.

One famous study conducted by UCLA psychologist Albert Mehrabian found that in highly emotional one-on-one conversations, words account for just 7 percent of how the other person will form an impression of you (38 percent comes from vocal tone and 55 percent comes from body language). That study can't be applied to media communications; your words will clearly account for more than just 7 percent of an audience's impression of you during most interviews. Still, that study is emblematic of a few larger truths about communications:

1. Your vocal tone and body language can enhance the effectiveness of your words, make you appear more credible, and allow the audience to forge a personal connection with you. If the audience likes you and relates to you, they will be more receptive to your message.

2. The audience won't be able to focus on your words if you're doing something with your voice or body that distracts them. They won't hear you if you constantly say "ummm," fail to maintain eye contact, or look defensive.

3. If your words are saying one thing and your body is saying another (what I call a "message disconnect"), the audience will believe what your body is telling them. Many speakers confuse their audiences with message disconnects without even knowing it. As an example, I often coach business executives who are preparing to announce a new product. A shocking percentage of them say something such as, "This is very exciting" while standing motionless and speaking in a monotone. It's easy to see why their audiences would conclude that the new product isn't even remotely exciting.

In the next few lessons, you will learn the most important elements of effective body language. You'll also see a few tips on managing your fear and dressing for success, which will help you project a more confident outward appearance.

49 ENERGY

After concluding on-camera practice interviews with our clients, I often ask them to rate how much energy they thought they had, on a scale of 1 to 10. "Oh, around an eight or nine," the trainees usually guess. "That was probably a bit over-the-top, right?"

I then ask the other people in the room to rate their colleagues' energy during the interview. They usually rate it a 4 or 5. The trainee is always shocked.

It turns out we're not great judges of the amount of energy we convey during media interviews. What feels right to clients in the training room often looks flat on television—which makes sense when you consider that television tends to make people appear more muted than they do in person.

You've seen that dynamic play out if you've ever sat down in front of your television, watched an entire interview, and completely zoned out—realizing later that you can't remember a single thing the spokesperson said. It happens all the time, and it's usually the result of a "blah" spokesperson who doesn't reach out of the television and grab you.

Apple founder Steve Jobs was known for his energetic delivery.

A media interview delivered without energy is like a steak cooked over low heat: dull, uninspiring, and lacking "sizzle." Great spokespersons know they need to inject passion and energy into their delivery to fully reach their audience.

Some of our clients get nervous about displaying too much energy or passion during their interviews. They protest that they're mild mannered or soft-spoken in everyday life and that speaking loudly wouldn't feel authentic to them. That's fine. Passionate need not be loud.

106

> *A media interview delivered without energy is like a steak cooked over low heat: dull, uninspiring, and lacking "sizzle."*

But what may feel like yelling to you usually doesn't come across as yelling to the rest of us. In fact, when I ask trainees to "go bigger" by speaking in a comically loud voice, they're almost always surprised to find that it goes over great on TV.

Therefore, focus on being the most energetic and passionate version of *you*. Think about when you're sitting in your living room with an old friend, reliving memories of your schooldays. You're probably a bit louder than usual, a little more demonstrative, and *a lot* more interesting.

In order to bring that more enthusiastic version of yourself out, try speaking 10—15 percent louder. Many people fear that will make them come across with too much volume. And sure, we need to dial back the occasional trainee who goes too far. But that's rare. The vast majority of the time, spokespersons can hit the gas and be even *more* energetic.

So don't hold back. If you care about your topic, make sure the audience can tell just by looking at you.

50 EYE CONTACT

Your eyes say a lot. Consider these common expressions:

"Is he staring at me?"

"I felt like she was looking right through me."

"He gazed lovingly into her eyes."

"Did that guy just give me the stink-eye?"

Your eyes say even more during television interviews, since tight shots of your face make them appear huge on TV screens.

According to Allan and Barbara Pease's *Definitive Book of Body Language,* Westerners maintain eye contact just 40—60 percent of the time when talking. That's probably a good thing, since anyone displaying an over-abundance of eye contact can appear downright creepy.

But the TV guest who maintains eye contact just 40—60 percent of the time will fail. Inconsistent eye contact communicates nervousness, defensiveness, even a lack of trustworthiness.

> *Inconsistent eye contact communicates nervousness, defensiveness, even a lack of trustworthiness.*

Aim for close to 100 percent eye contact. Keeping your eyes locked in a fixed position during an entire interview won't feel natural, since we often look away when trying to retrieve data from our brains (depending on the type of information, we look up, down, or to the side). But since great spokespersons do most of their thinking before the interview begins, there's no need for them to look anywhere but at their target.

There are generally three formats for television interviews:

1. **"Bites" Interviews:** This is the most common format, typically used by producers who intend to use only a few quotes, or sound bites, from your interview. You will look slightly off camera, lock eyes with the interviewer, and ignore the camera.

During bites interviews, look at
the interviewer, not the camera.

2. **On-Set Interviews:** This format, which is often seen on morning "chat" shows, most closely resembles everyday conversations. Lock eyes with the interviewer or whichever guest is speaking.

3. **Remote Interviews:** This is the most difficult format, since you have to stare directly into a camera. Before the interview begins, visualize your "target person." Act as if the camera is that person. Stare into the lens during your entire interview, even when you're not speaking—you might still appear on screen while you're listening. You can practice in advance by delivering your answers to a specific spot on your office wall.

If you're unsure which format will be used, just ask the producer where to look before the interview begins.

51 GESTURES

Many people tell me they were instructed by a previous media trainer never to gesture when they speak. A few were even taught—often by grade school teachers—that gesturing is rude.

That's terrible guidance. Your goal during a media interview is to appear as natural on camera as you are in person, and almost everyone gestures naturally when they speak. Sure, a small percentage of people gesture *too much*, but that's a rare problem.

According to body language experts Allan and Barbara Pease, "Using hand gestures grabs attention, increases the impact of communication, and helps individuals retain more of the information they are hearing."

In other words, gesturing not only helps you *look* more natural but also *enhances* the impact of your words.

We see that regularly in our media training sessions. When we encourage trainees to incorporate gestures into their delivery, something amazing happens: their *words* get better. The physical act of gesturing helps them form clearer thoughts and speak in tighter sentences.

To gesture effectively, keep your hands "unlocked" at all times—no clasped hands, hands behind your back, hands in pockets, or arms crossed in front of you. Those "closed" positions can communicate arrogance or defensiveness, and they lower the audience's ability to absorb and retain your information.

For seated interviews, keep your hands and arms unlocked and ready to gesture at any moment. When not gesturing, you can:

- Keep your hands on your lap near your knees.

- Nest your hands loosely within one another atop your lap.

Avoid clasping your hands or gripping your thighs, which can make you appear nervous (men should also be careful to steer clear of the defensive "hands covering groin" position).

Avoid all "closed" body language,
such as clasped hands.

For standing interviews, you have two good options:

- Loosely nest your hands, one within the other, keeping them at navel level when not gesturing.

- Rest your hands at your side, bringing them up to gesture (it feels strange, but looks fine to the audience).

If you're having a tough time gesturing naturally, speak about 10—15 percent louder than usual. As parents know all too well, it's impossible to yell at your kids while your hands and arms are frozen—an increase in volume helps to reanimate motionless hands.

Finally, some people wonder if they should still gesture if the television program on which they're appearing will only use a tight shot of their face, neck, and shoulders. Absolutely. Viewers can always tell if a spokesperson is gesturing—even if they can't see the movements—because the spokesperson's face is more expressive as a result.

52 POSTURE

Slump back into your chair for a moment.

Comfortable? Good. Now try to gesture enthusiastically.

If you're like most people, it isn't easy. Your gestures probably feel a bit forced and appear too casual for a media interview.

Now try something different: Shift forward so that your behind no longer touches the back of the chair. Plant your feet firmly on the floor in front of you. (Women may also opt to cross their feet at the ankles.)

Lean forward a bit. A slight angle is enough—any more than that and you'll look like you're about to lunge at the reporter (something we typically discourage, even if the journalist is particularly irksome).

Try to gesture again.

It's easier, right? Doesn't it feel more natural, more authentic, and less forced?

Many people sit for their media interviews in that slumped-back position (often with their legs crossed, another no-no), which inevitably dampens their energy and decreases their volume. Such a casual position can lead the public to conclude that those spokespersons are arrogant, unconcerned, or uncaring.

But one of the remarkable things about media training is watching the tremendous impact that "small" adjustments can make, and proper posture is chief among them. Simply by leaning forward a bit, spokespersons automatically have higher energy, increased volume, and more natural gestures.

Another "small" adjustment can help if your interview is conducted while standing instead of sitting: Place one foot just a few inches in front of the other. Doing so will help prevent the dreaded side-to-side sway and will keep your energy aimed forward, toward the lens (and thus, toward your audience).

This spokesperson does a great job of projecting his energy toward the audience.

It's worth noting that some people are great interviewees while standing but sleep-inducing while seated, and vice versa. If you're struggling with either seated or standing interviews, try the other. Since television crews occasionally have some flexibility in the way they shoot their interviews, it might be worth mentioning your preference for standing or sitting. They may not be able to accommodate your request, but it rarely hurts to ask.

For panel discussions, avoid slumping over the table. Lean forward just a touch, nest one hand loosely within the other and rest both hands on the table while not talking, and gesture while speaking. Better yet, work with conference planners to arrange for the panel to sit on stools in front of the audience rather than behind a table. You can tuck your legs behind you on the stool, but the rest of the posture rules for seated interviews still apply.

Finally, beware of swivel chairs. Spokespersons seated in chairs that twist predictably swing back and forth throughout the interview, so lock the chair or avoid it altogether.

53 VOICE

Most people don't have a monotone vocal delivery. That's the good news. The bad news is that most communicators use only a small portion of their available vocal range.

Our voices are incredible tools, capable of infusing great meaning into individual words and phrases. Simply by altering our volume, pitch, pace, and tone, we can better emphasize key points and help retain our audience's attention.

Imagine you're listening to the radio. The woman being interviewed is speaking at a moderate volume and average pace, but suddenly she slows down and almost whispers, "And right then, I knew I was in trouble." By changing her vocal pattern, she signaled to the audience that something important was coming. We tend to do that in everyday life when we're speaking with friends—and conversational is exactly what media interviews are supposed to *sound* like (even though they are *not* conversations).

Turn on a news radio station and listen to the way the anchors inject vocal variety into their verbal deliveries. Then practice for yourself by selecting a newspaper article and underlining a few key phrases that you want to emphasize verbally. Read the story aloud, and use your voice to highlight those phrases.

Keep these six things in mind for your vocal delivery:

1. **Volume:** Speaking loudly adds energy and excitement to your delivery, while speaking softly increases intimacy and drama.

2. **Pace:** Most people speak between 150 and 160 words per minute, but that number tends to increase when they get nervous. Speaking quickly can be useful if you're trying to add excitement to a specific point, but be careful not to rush through your entire interview. Speak a little slower than usual when

discussing more complicated information, emphasizing a key point, or building drama.

3. **Pitch:** When you ask a question, your pitch usually goes up at the end of the sentence; when you give a command, your pitch goes down. People tend to speak with a higher pitch when they're nervous or excited and with a lower pitch when they feel more relaxed and controlled. Both can be effective, but be careful to avoid vocal "upticks," which occur when your pitch gets higher at the end of every sentence. An uptick makes you sound as if you're seeking permission rather than making a statement—and too many of them will diminish your credibility.

4. **Tone:** Your tone adds emotion to words. For example, try saying aloud, "Sure, I love you," three different ways: sincerely, sarcastically, and sadly. Those versions each convey something different, and good speakers align their words with the tone they wish to convey.

5. **Silences:** Well-timed pauses can add drama to your vocal delivery or allow audiences an extra moment to consider your message. You can't be silent for long periods of time, but even a one-second pause can be incredibly effective immediately before or after making a key point.

6. **Diaphragmatic Breathing:** Take a deep breath. If your chest expands, you aren't breathing correctly. Try it again, but as you breathe *in*, push your stomach *out*. Make sure your chest doesn't move. Now begin talking and expending that air you've taken in. Your stomach should be moving in. That's "diaphragmatic breathing," and the benefits are enormous for the spoken word. Breathing properly makes your voice fuller, more resonant, and less nasal—and it gives you better breath control, meaning you won't have to gasp for air as often.

54 ELIMINATE THE "UHHHS" AND "UMMMS"

"Like, I don't know, the movie was, like, ummm, good, I guess, but, like, it wasn't, uhhh, awesome, you know?"

Do you know that teenager? If you've ever raised one or stood next to one at a shopping mall, you probably do.

Although that type of "verbal filler" is most commonly associated with teens, adults are guilty of using it as well. That's okay. Almost everyone uses at least some verbal filler while speaking, and it only becomes a problem when it distracts an audience. So don't be too self-critical if you utter the occasional "uhhh."

If you're concerned about verbal filler, these two tips may help:

1. ELIMINATING VERBAL FILLER AT THE BEGINNING OF AN ANSWER

Verbal filler that occurs at the beginning of your answer is usually the result of not having formed a complete thought before speaking. If the interview is live, pause for a moment before answering. That brief pause will help you structure your answer before delivering it to the audience.

It's even easier if the interview isn't live. The audience will rarely see your pauses in an edited interview, so take your time before answering a question—even if that means you pause for 5 or 10 seconds.

2. ELIMINATING VERBAL FILLER DURING AN ANSWER

Killing verbal filler that occurs in the middle of your answer is more challenging, but a technique I learned early in my career (I began as a small-town radio DJ) should help. My program director at the time was concerned that I uttered too many "ummms" on the air, so he taught me a useful technique to help me find a smooth radio delivery.

116

Here's how it works. Look around the room and find an object. Don't think about it. Just find an object and shout it out (example: "Printer!").

Begin speaking about that object for 30 seconds. Time it. You're not allowed to use "uhhhs" or "ummms," but you *are* allowed to pause briefly between sentences. Don't worry about the words you choose—just let them flow. My 30-second drill about the printer looked like this:

> *"I like my printer. I've had it for about two years, and it rarely jams, which I really appreciate as a busy person who runs his own business. It sits on the corner of my desk in my office in New York City. The best part of my office is the view of the Chrysler Building. It's pretty cool to sit, especially in the dark of winter, and see a Manhattan icon out my office window."*

You can practice this anywhere—in your car ("Ashtray!"), your shower ("Shampoo!"), and your office ("Burnt popcorn smell!"). The key is to surprise yourself with the object, speak aloud for 30 seconds, and replace *articulated* pauses with *silent* ones.

Many people think they've gotten through the drill with no verbal filler, but the audio replay might show they had two "likes" and a "ya know." So use your smartphone's "record" feature to ensure the verbal filler is really gone.

CASE STUDY: CAROLINE KENNEDY'S FAILED SENATE BID (V)

In 2009, New York's governor briefly considered Caroline Kennedy to fill a vacant Senate seat that opened when Hillary Clinton departed to become U.S. secretary of state.

Her interviews were disasters. According to *The Wall Street Journal*, she said "you know" 168 times during a single 30-minute interview. After being roundly mocked by the local press, Ms. Kennedy removed herself from consideration.

55 OVERCOMING FEAR

Most people experience nervousness during media interviews, and probably for the same reason—they don't want to make an embarrassing mistake that humiliates them in front of their peers and prevents them from achieving their goals.

There is no silver bullet for eliminating nervousness entirely. But you *can* learn how to manage your fear more effectively and lose some of the butterflies that hinder your performance.

Here are seven tips and techniques that have helped me—and thousands of our clients—over the past decade:

1. **Practice makes perfect:** Most people tell us that the single best way to reduce their fear is by getting familiar with their material and conducting several practice interviews in advance. (You'll read more about the best way to conduct a practice interview in lesson 98.) Our trainees also tell us that their fear recedes as they gain more media experience. Therefore, take every opportunity you can to practice with smaller media outlets before giving your first "big time" interview.

2. **But you don't have to *be* perfect:** No one is judging you on a scale of perfection. You're allowed to stumble over a phrase, say the occasional "ummm," or forget a word here and there. If you focus on doing the big things well—delivering quality content with passion—the audience is probably going to form a positive impression of you.

3. **Just because you feel it doesn't mean they see it:** You're a bad judge of your own nervousness. Don't assume the audience can sense your pounding heart or sweaty palms—they usually don't.

4. **Remember, it's not about you:** Stop focusing on your own fears and focus on the audience instead. Think about *their* lives, *their* needs, and *their* concerns. Remind yourself how your information can make *their* lives better. Try to serve *them*. It's not about you. It's about *them*.

5. **Stay in the moment:** If you make a mistake, stay in the moment. Don't beat yourself up while the interview is still in progress—if you lose your focus, you'll make additional mistakes and compound your original error. Self-flagellate after the interview ends if you must, but never during the interview.

6. **Take long, deep breaths:** Adults breathe an average of 12 times per minute. That number goes up when you get stressed, which leads to a reduced concentration of carbon dioxide in your blood and oxygen in your brain. Taking long, deep breaths can help you regain control of your respiration, so try this exercise shortly before your interview begins. Start by slowly exhaling all of the air from your lungs. Next, slowly inhale through your nose until your lungs are full. Hold your breath for as long as you can comfortably do so. Slowly release the air through your mouth until your lungs feel empty again. Repeat this exercise 10—12 times.

7. **Flex your muscles:** You can also use a modified version of a technique called "progressive muscle relaxation" by flexing—then releasing—different muscles. Sit in a comfortable chair and close your eyes. Flex the muscles in your face for 10 seconds, then relax for 20 seconds. Move on to your neck and repeat the same exercise, continuing on with your shoulders, then your arms, then your hands, then your chest, then your stomach, and downward until you reach your toes.

56 GENERAL RULES WHEN DRESSING FOR TELEVISION

Most people prefer to be judged on their words, not on their look. But there's no escaping the fact that your physical appearance on television is a critical part of your message.

"People *do* judge you during the first few seconds," author Lillian Brown notes in *Your Public Best: The Complete Personal Appearance and Media Training Guide*. "If your appearance is attractive, you can get an audience on your side before you have even said a word."

That may seem obvious, but it's more complicated than it sounds. Studio lights and camera lenses change the way we perceive people on our home television screens.

The consequences can be devastating. Few can recall what Richard Nixon said in the first televised presidential debate with John F. Kennedy in 1960, but many people remember how he looked. Mr. Nixon, who refused makeup, appeared pale and sweaty. Mr. Kennedy, who wore makeup, looked poised and comfortable. Americans who heard the debate on the radio concluded that Nixon had won; those who watched it on television sided with Kennedy.

Richard Nixon refused makeup in the 1960 presidential debate. His sweaty appearance stood in marked contrast to John F. Kennedy's more polished look.

Since viewers will judge your physical appearance before you've even said a word, carefully think through in advance what your look says about you. Keep these two general rules in mind:

1. **Be true to your brand:** It's crucial that your look is congruent with your brand. If you're representing a cutting-edge fashion house, don't dress like a scientist (unless it's the latest hipster look!), and vice versa. If you're representing an informal brand, you may dress casually, but should still look professional and thoughtfully put together.

2. **Look like yourself:** You should end up looking like yourself, with minor adjustments. Only if you're comfortable with your appearance will you be able to successfully put it out of your mind and radiate the self-confidence that will reinforce your message.

Tammy Faye Bakker, the late televangelist, is best remembered for her eccentric makeup.

In general, your wardrobe, makeup, and hairdo should be simple and understated so that they don't distract from the most expressive part of your face—your eyes—or from your words. In other words, avoid the Tammy Faye Bakker look if you want to be taken seriously.

57 ATTIRE

When dressing for television, don't get too fancy. Instead, Lillian Brown says, "Wear plain colors and patterns that don't 'do' anything."

Solid colors convey "more authority and sophistication than a print," advise Deborah Boland and JoJami Tyler, co-owners of the media- and image-consulting firm TV Image Live. But not all solids are created equal. "Pastels have always been flattering on TV, but the message they send is soft," Boland and Tyler say, so eschew them if you're in a hard-edged field such as finance or law. If you must wear prints, avoid patterns such as stripes, polka dots, and checks, all of which can appear to vibrate or shimmer on television.

For a speech he gave while running for president in 2012, Mitt Romney wore a solid suit, a solid shirt, and a broadly striped tie.

With the advent of high-definition (HD) television, there are no longer colors that are taboo on television (continue to avoid red, black, and white for non-HD videos). But white works best under a jacket so it doesn't wash out your face. And ask the producers if there are any caveats for their set—you wouldn't want to wear a green suit on a show with a green background, for example.

Such considerations aside, you typically can't go wrong with most grays, blues, or brown-based earth tones. But add a bit of variety. "High color contrast makes you look sharper and more authoritative than monochromatic looks," say Boland and Tyler.

Men's suits should hang well, and their hems should be long enough to avoid exposing your legs while seated. Wear long, dark socks. Choose an understated tie without conspicuous patterns, bright colors, or shiny materials (two good options are red ties that can provide some useful visual punch, or a more subtle color that is similar to your eye color). Make sure your shirt collar, which frames the lower part of your face, fits well.

Women should pay attention to their necklines. "A V-neck or scoop-neck top on a woman is more flattering and makes you look slimmer," say Boland and Tyler. "If you think a top may be too low cut, it is."

Some additional guidelines apply equally to men and women: long sleeves appear more formal than short sleeves, shoes should always be shined, and it's best to choose natural fabrics or blends that conform easily to the body. For both clothes and accessories, avoid items that make noise when you move, and stick to things with low sheen. One of Brown's tricks: look in the mirror with your eyes half-closed; if something outshines you, take it off. Lapel pins may seem unobtrusive, but they may flash on screen and, unless they're very common symbols, leave people guessing about their meaning. They're best avoided.

Before you go on air, brush your lapels and shoulders if there's any chance they may be adorned with dandruff, pet hair, or baby spit-up. And unbutton your jacket's bottom button when you sit down, in order to keep the lapels straight. Jackets will also look better if you tuck the ends under you when you sit. Most important, you should feel comfortable. For that reason, don't wear an outfit for the first time during an interview.

58 MAKEUP

"Makeup has only one purpose: to enhance your natural beauty," writes Lillian Brown. "It should maximize your good features and subtly diminish any problem areas. Your makeup should be a miracle of understatement and should not attract attention to itself."

Both men and women need to wear makeup on television, because bright lights and powerful camera lenses cast unflattering shadows and expose the tiniest imperfections.

If you're appearing on a national show or in a top media market, you may have access to a makeup artist before you go on-air; otherwise, you're on your own. You can buy everything you need at the nearest drugstore, but consider consulting an expert (a cosmetics-counter staffer at a department store should be fine) who can help you pick out the most flattering shades and teach you how to apply them properly.

Although makeup is a very individual matter, there are some general guidelines. Pay most attention to your skin and eyes. "If your eyes show up and your skin looks good, you'll look pretty good," says Rebecca Perkins, head of the makeup department for *Law & Order: SVU*.

Both men and women should fix shadows under their eyes, use powder to eliminate shine, and avoid using moisturizer on their faces before an appearance.

Men should cover up their whisker area using a "base and powder" from a compact, and absorb perspiration with a tissue or astringent.

Women should use foundation that has a natural finish (avoid shimmer) and perfectly matches their skin tone. Use a lighter shade under the eyes and a darker one for subtle contours. Take great care to blend it into your neck to avoid dramatic lines.

*Professional makeup artists can make you look
terrific, but you can still look great without one.*

Make sure your brow is nicely tweezed and your eyes are well defined. Perkins's advice: Use very thin eyeliner and/or high-quality mascara. Unless you're dark skinned, stick with browns rather than blacks and grays, says Ingrid Grimes-Miles, the makeup artist who created Michelle Obama's clean look and works for WGN-TV's morning show in Chicago.

If you wear eye shadow, she recommends choosing a soft, natural shade and blending it well. "Stay away from smoky eyes, even if you're proficient at it," Grimes-Miles adds, "because you don't know how that camera will pick it up."

Use a lipstick shade that is similar to the color of the inside of your mouth. Make sure the lip-pencil line is not visible, and avoid gloss.

If you're fortunate enough to be appearing on a show with a makeup artist, hedge your bets. "Always show up to the station camera-ready so you're not surprised should a makeup person not be available to you," Grimes-Myles says. It's fine to bring your favorite products, but remember they're the experts and are intimately familiar with their studio's lighting and cameras.

59 HAIR

Think of your hair as a frame around your face, advises Lillian Brown in *Your Public Best: The Complete Personal Appearance and Media Training Guide*. Like a good frame, it should flatter without drawing undue attention. You can achieve this with a modern cut (no Farrah Fawcett flip, for instance) that doesn't fall into your eyes. Allow three-quarters of an inch clearance around the eyes to compensate for shadows.

Former first lady Laura Bush kept her hair away from her eyes in this official portrait.

"A little volume is always good," so use a brush instead of a comb, say Deborah Boland and JoJami Tyler, co-owners of TV Image Live.

"If you color your hair," Boland and Tyler say, "make sure it's not a solid blob of color. Especially with blondes, have your hairdresser use two or three different-colored blonde highlights to make it look natural. Warmer blondes look better on camera than cooler tones."

Hairstyles that look best on men are those that cover the top halves of their ears and reach down almost to the collar in the back. Make sure no stray hairs are sticking up, and keep beards and mustaches well trimmed and off the lips.

Unless your hair is a key part of your image,
avoid pop star Justin Bieber's early look.

What if hair is a distant memory? Baldness can look fine on television as long as you minimize the shine. Apply a little powder and keep your jaw level to the floor to avoid dominating the picture with your pate. And stay out of the sun beforehand, unless you want a sunburned forehead to be all that viewers remember.

One final caveat: Avoid getting a haircut just before your appearance. It will look more natural if you get it cut a few days before your interview.

Comb down the stragglers, unless you want to
look like boxing promoter Don King.

60 DRESSING FOR HIGH-DEFINITION TELEVISION

Aside from your clothes, makeup, and hair, there are several other aspects of your physical appearance to consider before going on television. And there are some general things worth bearing in mind for today's high-definition shows.

Your hands may show up on camera, so apply a little makeup base on age spots and make sure your nails are well tended. Clear, pink-tinged, or flesh-colored nail polish shades work best.

If you wear glasses, choose frames and lenses that don't draw unwanted attention. Avoid shiny or brightly colored frames, and make sure the glasses don't obscure your brows or dominate your other features.

Former talk show host Sally Jesse Raphael is known for wearing oversized red glasses.

One tried-and-true method is to choose a frame that matches your hair. Apply some cream makeup or powder onto shiny frames to minimize their reflected glare. It's best to have glare-resistant lenses and to steer clear of tinted lenses. If you're deciding between glasses and contacts, wear whichever makes you feel more comfortable.

As for high-definition television, remember that commercial where people watching a golf tournament at home could spot the golf ball way off in the distance even though the people on the green couldn't find it? It's not too far off the mark. "Things that show up in real life show up much more in HD," says Rebecca Perkins, head of the makeup department for *Law & Order: SVU.*

There are different types of high definition, so a lot depends on the camera and the filters being used, as well as the technical skills of the camera operator and the lighting designer.

Regardless of the technical setup, remember one critical rule of thumb when dressing for HD: keep your wardrobe and makeup subtle. Something considered "bright" in real life might look "a little crazy" on an HD television monitor, Perkins says.

> *Keep your wardrobe and makeup subtle. Something considered "bright" in real life might look "a little crazy" in HD.*

It's even more important in HD to blend makeup very carefully to avoid obvious contrast lines, advises Ingrid Grimes-Miles, from WGN-TV's morning show in Chicago. And if anyone tells you that powder should be avoided in this format, ignore them. "You absolutely do need powder, otherwise you will come across oily," Grimes-Miles says.

Textures are also much more pronounced in HD, so go with smooth and natural ones. And double-check that your clothes are literally spotless. "If you wear a dark color, swipe your shoulders before you go on," caution image consultants Deborah Boland and JoJami Tyler.

SECTION SIX

The Different Media Formats

"Societies have always been shaped more by the nature of the media by which men communicate than by the content of the communication."

Marshall McLuhan, Canadian scholar

61 EMAIL INTERVIEWS

Many spokespersons prefer to do media interviews by email, since the format feels familiar and removes some of the unpredictability of a telephone or in-person interview.

Email interviews have their place. For example, you might conduct an interview by email when:

- You have an existing relationship with the reporter.

- The reporter is seeking technical information that is more easily communicated in writing.

- The reporter needs a quick answer to a straightforward question, is facing a bruising deadline, or is clarifying something you said in an earlier interview.

- The reporter prefers to do the interview by email.

- Logistical issues prevent speaking by phone or in person.

- The correspondence is about a *highly controversial* issue, and you must maintain a paper trail for legal reasons.

While email interviews can be useful, they are too often used by controlling executives and nervous spokespersons who do everything possible to avoid picking up the phone. Don't do interviews by email simply because it makes you more comfortable; doing so can be counterproductive. Here are three reasons to avoid making email interviews a habit:

1. **They preclude useful conversation:** Good reporters listen to your answers closely in order to ask informed follow-up questions. Those follow-ups are often helpful to your cause—they can help you gauge the reporter's perspective, clarify incorrect points, and add context to your message.

2. **They prevent personal relationships:** Media relations is about relationships, which are especially important when you're accused of wrongdoing. Reporters who know you are more likely to give you the benefit of the doubt, reducing the risk of negative stories and improving the tone of coverage.

3. **They appear obstructionist (sometimes):** The medium in which you choose to communicate often says a lot. If you respond to a controversial topic by email, the reporter may say, "In a written statement, Company X said..." That may look obstructionist to the audience, especially if your critics were willing to speak to the reporter. The contrast of *their* willingness to talk and *your* "email-only" approach may make your critics appear more credible.

THE POWER OF UNINTENDED MEANINGS

A clever book called *The Lexicon of Intentionally Ambiguous Recommendations* lists dozens of things employers can say to people who call for references on lousy former employees.

To describe a **lazy** candidate, you can say, "In my opinion, you will be very fortunate to get this person to work for you."

To describe an **unproductive** candidate, it suggests, "I can assure you that no person would be better for the job."

And to describe a person with **lackluster** credentials, it recommends, "All in all, I cannot say enough good things about this candidate or recommend him too highly."

Email interviews carry the same risk of unintended meanings (which are often less likely to occur in person, since your vocal emphasis and body language help your points come across more clearly). Show your typed responses to a few people before sending them, and parse every word to ensure you haven't given the reporter a quote you'll come to regret.

62 PHONE INTERVIEWS

Most people don't know how to use a telephone. Sure, they talk on the phone with their family, friends, and business contacts every day. But the telephone habits they use during those calls are radically different from the ones they need for print or radio interviews conducted by phone, known as "phoners."

So forget everything you (think) you know and remember these eight tips the next time you have a phoner:

1. **Get out of your office:** Don't sit at your desk, where you can become easily distracted by incoming emails, phone calls, and office visitors. Find an empty conference room with no distractions, and tape a "Do Not Disturb—Interview in Progress" sign on the door.

2. **Bring your notes:** It's okay to have notes in front of you during phone interviews. Be careful not to "read" them to the reporter but to use them only as memory triggers. (See lesson 94 for more about the best way to prepare notes for an interview.)

3. **Get a headset:** Telephone headsets are terrific gadgets for phone interviews. They allow you to use both of your hands to gesture, which adds emphasis to your voice, and they free you from cradling a phone to your neck in case you need to jot down a few notes during your call.

4. **Stand:** When our trainees stand, they literally "think faster on their feet." They also tend to project more authority, likely because pacing helps them use their nervous energy in a more productive manner.

5. **Smile:** Smile when appropriate. The reporter (and audience, for radio interviews) can hear your warmth radiating through the phone.

6. **Prioritize audio quality:** Speaker and cell phones have inferior sound quality and can be a barrier to easy communication. Plus, reporters may conclude, "He thinks he's too important to pick up the damn phone?" It's best to use a landline with a high-quality headset.

7. **Click, clack, repeat:** During print interviews, listen for the sound of typing on the other end—you'll hear it when you say something that intrigues the reporter. That's your cue to slow down and repeat what you've just said to make sure the reporter has time to capture every word. Also, don't hesitate to check in with the reporter by asking whether your explanation made sense.

8. **Now, what did I just say?** If you think you may have mangled a key quote, you can ask the reporter to read it back to you (some reporters will oblige, others won't). Reporters may not be willing to change something you said if you don't like the way you said it—but they usually will if you said something factually inaccurate.

CASE STUDY: TORONTO MAYOR'S DISASTROUS PHONE INTERVIEW (V)

In 2010, Toronto Mayor-Elect Rob Ford agreed to an interview with *As It Happens*, a national radio program that airs on the CBC (Canadian Broadcasting Corporation).

But when the reporter called at the scheduled time, Mr. Ford was busy coaching a youth football game. He proceeded with the interview anyway.

Unsurprisingly, he was unfocused, simultaneously yelling at children and telling the reporter about fiscal restraint. He interrupted the interview numerous times and made his points inarticulately, until finally admitting he was "being distracted."

The interview ran unedited, creating an embarrassing—and self-inflicted—public relations disaster for the incoming mayor.

63 RADIO: SEVEN WAYS TO ROCK YOUR NEXT INTERVIEW

I've done hundreds of radio interviews throughout my career. They *seem* simple. After all, you just pick up a phone or visit a studio and have a conversation with the host.

But radio interviews are nothing like normal conversations (unless your friends take listener phone calls and toss to a commercial break every few minutes!). Remember these seven rules for your next radio interview:

1. **Prepare for an abrupt start:** Most radio interviews are done by phone, not in studio, and most stations prefer to call you rather than have you call into the studio (it can work either way). Some producers call a few minutes before the interview begins, allowing you to listen for few minutes to get a feel for the program's tone. But others wait until the last possible second, meaning you're on the air within moments of picking up the phone. When you pick up the phone, be ready to go live on a second's notice—or on no notice at all. You'll hear the host over the phone line, so turn your radio off to avoid hearing a distracting delay.

2. **Express passion:** Sure, you're on the radio. But listeners will hear it if you stand, move your hands, and smile—so get a telephone headset and gesture away. Try to match or slightly exceed the host's energy level to avoid sounding flat.

3. **Sit close to the microphone (in studio):** Ari Ashe, a reporter and producer for Washington, DC's top-rated WTOP-FM, advises guests to sit close to the microphone, no farther than a "fist's-length" away.

4. **Connect with the host (in studio):** Mr. Ashe says it's key for radio guests to make eye contact. "Look at the interviewer," he

says. "Speak to him or her, and speak like you're talking to a friend or spouse. If you exude confidence and comfort with the interviewer, the listener will feel confident and comfortable with you. Be friendly, be cordial, and act like you're just chatting with your best friend." It's okay to take a few notes with you and glance down occasionally to remember your key points, but try not to lose your connection.

5. **Don't depend on them to make the plug:** You're probably on the radio because you want to promote something—a new book, your website, your company. Although many experienced hosts are adept at "plugging" whatever you want promoted, some aren't. So it's up to you to mention that information a few times throughout the interview. You can increase the host's odds of getting it right by sending in advance the information you'd like plugged. I also often send the producer a shortened version of my bio, which many hosts use verbatim to introduce me on the air.

6. **Treat crazy callers with respect:** If you appear on a radio show that takes listener calls, you may get an angry caller who goes on a rant that has little to do with your topic. Maintain the high ground. The public recognizes angry callers for what they are, so impress the audience with your graceful and kind handling of the caller. Push back on incorrect assertions, but do so respectfully.

7. **Listen to the tape:** Few people enjoy listening to tapes of their interviews, but doing so can help you identify and fix problem areas. At one point in my career, I was surprised to hear that I said "uhhh" a few too many times during my interviews. That self-awareness allowed me to kill the "uhhhs," eliminating a problem I otherwise wouldn't have known existed.

64 RADIO: FIVE THINGS BAD GUESTS DO

Radio stations hate boring guests, since they send listeners racing for the "off" button. In this lesson, two radio pros give you their takes on the five habits of bad radio guests.

1. **They give long answers:** Short answers allow the host to ask another question, take another phone call, or throw to commercial—so keep your answers to 30 seconds or less. Finish your answer with a declarative sentence that ends on a vocal downtick to make it clear to the host that you've completed your answer.

    Radio reporter Ari Ashe describes one particularly vexing radio guest:

    "WTOP once had a regular guest on from The Hill newspaper. Every interview went three minutes long and was exactly one question long. He went on and on, never stopping, never pausing, never letting our anchor get in a follow-up question. Our assistant news director talked to him. Nothing would change. We would talk to him again. Nothing would change. Eventually, we dropped him as a guest. We were no longer willing to put up with three-minute answers that would have been five minutes had we not cut him off. If you're looking to deliver a long-winded, dry speech, become a policy wonk. You won't succeed in radio with that strategy."

2. **They give complex answers:** Radio interviews are not college lectures, and your goal is not to tell the audience everything you know about a topic. Mr. Ashe compares wonky guests to his undergraduate organic chemistry teacher:

    "He could not present the material in a way that was easy to understand; it felt like he was speaking a foreign language. He couldn't explain difficult concepts in simple terms that

*connected to our everyday lives. Your job is to be a good teacher.
If you're like my organic chemistry teacher, you will not be
successful in radio."*

3. **They're boring:** Radio requires energy. Too many guests put
   a premium on the *quality* of their information but not nearly
   enough on their *delivery* of it. Great information is vital but
   isn't sufficient on its own. As Ashe says:

   *"Who wants to listen to someone who is putting them to
   sleep? Nobody! And when most of our listeners are driving,
   that's potentially dangerous. To win on radio, you must be
   memorable."*

4. **They're alarmist:** Ashe reminds radio guests not only to articulate the problem but also to offer solutions:

   *"Who wants to hear someone tell us life is terrible and you're
   doomed to suffer? Every problem has a solution and everyone
   wants to know what it is. If your attitude is that there are no
   solutions, people will tune out."*

5. **They leave their humor behind:** Some radio formats are lighter
   than others. And almost nothing is worse for a humorous host
   than a guest who refuses to play along. Bob Andelman, host
   of Mr. Media Interviews (unrelated to my Mr. Media Training
   Blog), says, "Little is worse than if I make a joke and there's
   silence." Unless humor is inappropriate for your topic, bring
   your sense of humor to an interview. That doesn't mean you
   have to be a comedian—it just means you have to be willing
   to play along.

65 TELEVISION: 10 THINGS YOU NEED TO KNOW

Appearing on television can be an odd experience. In one of the stranger (but more common) formats, you may be escorted to a closet-size booth, in which you will speak into a camera operated by a technician hundreds of miles away.

This lesson will help strip away some of the mystery by arming you with 10 logistical and technical details you'll need to know.

1. **Arrive early:** Avoid unnecessary stress by allowing plenty of extra time. That buffer will be valuable if the producer, makeup artist, or crew is running behind when you arrive. Plus, you may meet some interesting people in the "green room," the room in which you'll wait prior to the start of your interview.

2. **Bring makeup:** Most major networks and some larger local stations provide a makeup artist. Ask in advance whether you will have access to one, but bring your own makeup and hair products either way, just to be safe.

3. **Look in the mirror:** Do a final check in the mirror before your interview begins. I've seen guests with lipstick smeared on their teeth, big chunks of food stuck in-between teeth, and even an open sore (yes, really!).

4. **Check your microphone and test your earpiece:** You will often wear a lapel microphone during your interview. The wires should be hidden—men and women can run the cord beneath their tops; men can also tape the cord to the back of their tie. Make sure the microphone isn't brushing up against clothing or jewelry, which will make you sound muffled. You may also be fitted with an earpiece, or IFB (which stands for interruptible feedback). Test the audio before your interview begins and tell the crew immediately if the volume isn't quite right.

5. **Turn off your cell phone:** Little is more distracting than a cell phone ringing in middle of an interview. Also, the phone's signal can interfere with the audio. Vibrate mode isn't good enough; power your phone completely off.

6. **Turn the monitor off:** Television monitors in the studio often show a feed that is delayed by a fraction of a second. That can be extremely distracting, so ask the crew to turn off any monitors or to turn them away.

7. **Beware the split screen:** In some formats, you will appear on camera even when you're not speaking. Those "split screen" shots show you and at least one other person at the same time, and "reaction" shots show your reaction to another guest's comments. Act as if you're always on, being careful not to wipe your face, adjust your hair, or fix your outfit during your segment.

8. **Restrict your nodding:** It's normal to nod when listening to someone else, but nodding can send the wrong message if you disagree with the premise of someone's question or comment. Listen attentively, but only nod along if you agree.

9. **Avoid (or preplan) props:** We've all seen that television guest who holds up a piece of paper or newspaper article during a television appearance. It's usually a bad idea. Few people know how to position an item properly for the camera, so it usually ends up distracting the audience. If you want to show something during your interview, talk to the producer first. The producer can help the crew prepare for the shot in advance.

10. **Stay in your seat:** Avoid the temptation to flee your chair the moment your segment ends. Maintain your pose for a few seconds, remaining seated until a member of the crew tells you you're clear.

66 TELEVISION: KNOW YOUR BACKGROUND

What will show up behind you when you appear on television?

That decision is usually left up to television producers when interviews are held at their studios—but you may have significant control over your background for interviews conducted in the field, at your home, or at your office.

A thoughtfully selected background can enhance and reinforce your words, while a carelessly selected one can thoroughly undermine your message.

Politicians are among the most image-conscious, often conducting interviews and delivering speeches in front of a row of flags, banners bearing a campaign slogan ("For a Brighter Future," "Lower Taxes"), or iconic landmarks.

CASE STUDY: A NEGATIVE STORY
THE WHITE HOUSE LOVED

While covering the White House in the 1980s, CBS News reporter Lesley Stahl aired a scathing six-minute piece about President Reagan's broken promises.

In her book, *Reporting Live,* Ms. Stahl writes: "I knew the piece would have an impact...I worried that my sources at the White House would be angry enough to freeze me out."

But rather than freezing her out, Deputy Chief of Staff Dick Darman called to thank her. He was delighted with the *visuals* in the piece, which portrayed an optimistic president.

"Nobody heard what you said," he said. "You guys in Televisionland haven't figured it out, have you? When the pictures are powerful and emotional, they override if not completely drown out the sound. I mean it, Lesley. Nobody heard you."

Nonpoliticians should apply the same degree of thought by choosing backgrounds that reinforce their spoken messages.

Company representatives might stand on a bustling factory floor to show their business's vitality. Marine biologists might remove their shoes and deliver an interview from the water's edge. A health expert discussing the seriousness of diabetes might choose to do an interview from a local hospital's emergency room.

Your background is even more important during a crisis. As a general rule of thumb, don't display your logo during a crisis. Why *help* the audience remember that your brand is associated with bad news? That means you shouldn't stand in front of any signs, buildings, or awnings that feature your company's symbol. Also avoid wearing any clothing, caps, or pins that bear your company's name.

CASE STUDY: SARAH PALIN'S BLOODY THANKSGIVING (V)

After losing her bid for the vice presidency in 2008, Sarah Palin returned to Alaska to continue serving her term as governor.

As one of her ceremonial duties that November, she visited a local farm to pardon a turkey for Thanksgiving.

But when she gave a lighthearted interview to a local television station, she failed to check her background. Behind her, a man covered in blood was slaughtering turkeys by placing them into a grinder.

The media loved the gruesome video—some of which was too graphic to show on television—and played the clip for days. The coverage reinforced the media's narrative (fairly or not) of a politician unprepared for the national limelight.

67 LIVE VS. EDITED

Imagine you're on radio or television. You suddenly lose your train of thought. Is it a bad idea to abruptly stop and say, "Wait. I messed that up. Can I start over again?"

Not necessarily. The answer depends on the *format* of your interview. This lesson will look at the three most common interview formats: live, live-to-tape, and edited.

1. **Live:** Although live interviews terrify many media guests, they offer spokespersons the advantage of allowing the audience to see the full exchange and not having their words unfairly edited. On the other hand, you usually can't stop in middle of a live interview to restart an answer you blew the first time.

2. **Live-to-Tape:** These interviews are prerecorded but air unedited, so it's best to treat them as if they are live. Still, it's a good idea to ask the reporter before you begin whether you can stop if you make a mistake during the interview. Some reporters may be willing to start over or do minimal editing to correct an error in one of your responses.

3. **Edited:** Almost all print interviews are edited, as are radio and television programs that run short clips rather than full interviews. During edited interviews, you can stop and restart answers you didn't deliver to your satisfaction the first time. Although most interviewers will use the better version of your quote, they *can* use your less polished first answer if they desire, especially if you said something dramatic (or committed a seven-second stray; see lesson 35).

Additional rules apply to edited interviews since the audience will only read, hear, or see a small portion of your comments.

During edited interviews, don't say:

- **"As I mentioned earlier" or "as I've already said"** – In edited interviews, the audience won't necessarily hear what you said earlier, so banish these phrases from your media lexicon. Treat every answer as an independent, stand-alone response, and simply repeat what you said earlier (using different words). Plus, these types of phrases often come across in a way that makes the speaker sound slightly annoyed or mildly hostile.

- **"A, B, and C," "One, two, and three," or "First of all"** – Lists of numerous items usually take too much time to deliver in a single quote. Unless you can deliver the full list in a few short seconds, avoid these altogether.

- **"In conclusion" or "in summary"** – The audience may never hear what came before your summary, so just state your conclusion without inserting these phrases.

- **"Yesterday," "today," or "tomorrow"** – If you tape an interview that won't be aired the same day, you'll confuse the audience by saying "today." Unless you know precisely when the interview will air (and that it won't be re-aired at a later date), use the actual date instead.

- **The reporter's name** – Many radio and television interviews are conducted by a producer or an off-air reporter, not by the anchor or correspondent you'll hear on the radio or see on the screen. If you say the name of your interviewer during a key answer, the public will have no clue who you're talking about—and your quote will likely get dropped from the story. Unless you're sure that the person doing the interview will be the one appearing on the air, avoid using the reporter's name. Even then, it might be best just to skip it altogether.

68 LONG INTERVIEWS AND FEATURES

Most of the techniques in this book apply for short and long interviews alike. But if your interview will be longer than most— for example, a one-hour radio interview or a series of interviews for a "feature story"—you may need to make a few adjustments.

LONG INTERVIEWS

If you're invited onto a local radio program for a full hour, do you have to remain "on message" the whole time, or does the longer format allow you more flexibility than a quick three-minute interview does? Can you stray from your messages so you can cover more ground and introduce a few secondary points?

Some spokespersons conclude that they can, but it's a bad idea. Many radio and television stations have a high turnover rate, meaning that the people listening at the beginning of your interview may not be there at the end. Some people will catch just a few minutes in the middle of your interview, while others will tune into the final two minutes. If you only articulate your messages once or twice during the hour, many people will never hear your most important points.

But since some listeners *will* tune in for the entire hour, you can't simply repeat the same words throughout the interview. That's not a problem: if you prepare for media interviews as this book suggests, you'll be armed with about 20 messages and supports (stories, statistics, and sound bites) that will allow you to articulate your themes in many different ways during the hour.

There *is* one difference between long and short interviews: your answers can be a bit longer in an extended format. You can add additional detail to your stories and place your statistics into greater context. Still, keep your answers to one minute or less. Long-form media interviews are not an excuse to filibuster.

FEATURE INTERVIEWS

If you're deemed interesting enough or successful enough, reporters may want to profile you as the focus of an in-depth "feature" story. Features, sometimes known as personal profiles, are more commonly the province of newspapers, magazines, and websites, but some broadcasters also air them. Feature reporters often spend hours, days, or even weeks with their subjects in an effort to learn the most fascinating (or offbeat) things about them that they can.

For features, reporters will ask personal questions to learn more about your background—your place of birth, your educational and professional history, your marital status, your hobbies, what you've learned from your mistakes, your future goals, and more.

When answering those biographical questions, you're usually not on message. That's okay. Answering a question about your family life by saying you have a spouse and a child isn't going to cause harm. But remain wary of saying anything that can make you look unusually quirky or that undercuts your message.

CASE STUDY: "NONPARTISAN" LEADER VOTES REPUBLICAN

A former client, the head of a nonpartisan nonprofit group, was interviewed for a feature story in his hometown paper.

The reporter asked if he had an opinion about an upcoming election. Our client said he preferred the Republican candidate since he didn't trust the Democrat. His answer, which was included in the final story, undercut the public perception of his "nonpartisan" leadership.

He should have declined to answer the question and said he wasn't going to discuss his personal politics, since his obligation was to represent the nonpartisan group.

69 PRESS CONFERENCES: AN INTRODUCTION

Press conferences aren't as common as they used to be. Technology has allowed companies to disseminate information to reporters (and the public) without gathering the press in a single place—and that's a good thing, since reporters have less time than ever to leave their desks to attend a press conference (and many won't).

Still, press conferences *can* play an essential role in media communications, particularly for major news announcements, in political campaigns, and during crises.

Press conferences can be tricky, since reporters from competitive news organizations often play a game of one-upmanship to see who can ask the most difficult question. For that reason, press conferences—especially those about controversial or challenging topics—require a deft spokesperson. Ask yourself whether a press conference is truly the best way to release information before scheduling one.

If you decide to proceed with a press conference, here are four rules to remember:

1. **Test the logistics:** I've attended dozens of press conferences in which the spokesperson walks to the lectern, shuffles his papers, pats his finger on the microphone to test the volume, and looks around for a place to rest his water. When I see a press conference begin that way, it's a sure sign I'm in for a snoozer.

    You'd be surprised how many people fail to check the logistics before reporters arrive. Get there early, position the microphone to a comfortable height and test the volume, check the PowerPoint and its remote control, position your papers, and place a glass of room-temperature water within reach.

2. **State your name:** Begin the press conference by stating (and spelling) your name and giving reporters your preferred title.

Identifying yourself at the beginning helps ensure that broadcast journalists get your on-screen ID (known as a chyron) right.

3. **Coordinate with your co-presenters:** Little is more awkward than watching co-presenters fumble while transitioning to one another. Good co-presenters are like teammates in a relay race; one hands the baton off to the other seamlessly.

    Upon finishing the first portion of the press conference, a presenter should conclude with a line that wraps up the section and introduces the next speaker's part, such as, "Now that you have a better understanding of how our company intends to roll out this product, Joanne Myers, our lead researcher, is going to explain some of the science behind it."

    For the question-and-answer period, coordinate with your co-presenters in advance to determine which types of questions each of you will answer. While you might handle the business questions, for example, Joanne will take the lead on answering the scientific ones.

4. **Maintain eye contact:** If multiple cameras are present, keep eye contact with the questioner while answering the question. That way, every camera—regardless of its position—will show you delivering your answer with steady eye contact in one direction rather than darting purposelessly from one person to another.

The next lesson will deal with another critical decision you'll need to make when holding a press conference: whether to take questions or just make a statement.

70 PRESS CONFERENCES: OPENING STATEMENT AND QUESTIONS

During press conferences, should you take questions or avoid them altogether? This lesson will look at two of the most common press-conference formats and help you select the most appropriate one for different types of media announcements.

MAKING A STATEMENT WITHOUT TAKING QUESTIONS

Reporters rarely appreciate being denied the opportunity to ask questions at press conferences, and your refusal to answer their queries may result in negative coverage. But there are times when refusing questions is appropriate, especially in the very early stages of a crisis when little information is known. In those cases, your statement might look something like this:

> *"About 45 minutes ago, a Montgomery County school bus overturned on the Rockville Pike just north of Montrose Road in Rockville, Maryland. We know there were children on the bus, but we do not yet know how many or whether there are any injuries. Emergency crews are on the scene. Many school buses use that route, so I am not able to confirm which school the bus was headed for. I know a lot of parents watching this are anxiously awaiting more information, and we're doing everything we can to track that information down for them. I'm not going to take questions now because I want to continue gathering information for you. As soon as I know more, I'll come back to share it with you and will also post it to our website and social media feeds. Thank you."*

MAKING AN OPENING STATEMENT FOLLOWED BY QUESTIONS

Most press conferences fall into this category. Begin the press conference with a short statement containing the key facts and your main messages. Opening remarks typically run no more than 10 to 15 minutes, but press conferences about more technical topics often require a longer introductory statement. On the other hand, opening statements at the beginning of major crises might only run a minute or two.

When you finish your introductory statement (but before you open the floor to questions), tell reporters that you have a specific amount of time available to answer questions. In the early stages of a crisis, you might only allot five to ten minutes for questions; if you're launching a new product, you might allow an hour. By announcing the time available at the outset, you won't look like you're abruptly ending the gathering when you call for the last question. That's especially helpful if you're being barraged by hostile questions—because you already announced your intention to end the question period after an allotted time, you can't be accused of leaving in haste.

Count down the remaining time once or twice during the press conference. You might say, "I see we have five minutes left. Let's see if we can get in two more questions." Control the floor. Don't allow reporters to shout questions at the same time—choose the next questioner by calling on a reporter who is raising his or her hand. Don't allow one reporter to monopolize the time. After you've answered a reporter's question (and possibly a follow-up), offer to answer additional questions for that reporter after the press conference ends. Then move on to another questioner.

If you end the press conference before reporters have exhausted their questions, consider staying afterward to answer any remaining queries. But try to speak to only one reporter at a time—you can set up a small room in advance that accommodates just two people. If you allow a group of reporters to gather around you after the formal press conference ends, you'll essentially have another, less formal one on your hands.

As in other forms of media interviewing, you can use the ATMs to answer difficult questions. And since reporters are often more dangerous in groups, do everything possible to avoid a defensive tone. Once they smell blood, you're in trouble.

71 SOCIAL MEDIA: AN INTRODUCTION

Many of the executives we work with are terrified of social media. They've either experienced the dark side of it personally or heard horror stories from their industry peers: tales of vicious comments on an influential blogger's website; incorrect and badly damaging rumors on Twitter; or an embarrassing, secretly filmed video uploaded onto YouTube.

Those potential hazards are real. But executives tend to focus disproportionately on the downsides of social media and not nearly enough on the potential upsides. Their focus on the risks leads them to adopt a "head in sand" strategy of neglecting social media, which rarely works, at least in the long-term.

Social media—which include blogs, social networks, and video-sharing sites—offer today's communicators a tremendous advantage over their predecessors.

Think back for a moment to the turn of the 21st century, when journalists still dominated as the primary gatekeepers of information. If a company wanted media attention, it would send a press release to a few reporters and wait passively as the reporters decided whether or not to cover the story. Even if the company's work *was* covered, there was no guarantee of the story being favorable. Companies were at the mercy of the press.

To be sure, those reporters remain critical allies today. Positive stories by the media still bestow valuable third-party credibility onto you, while negative stories can diminish your reputation.

But the traditional media's influence is waning. Social media have flattened the playing field, allowing companies to disseminate the information they want, to whomever they want, whenever and however they want. There's no longer a need to wait for a journalist to file a story—if companies want their audiences to know something, they can just post it to their blog, Facebook page, or Twitter feed.

If you're still deciding whether or not to maintain a social media presence, the answer should almost surely be yes. Your audiences aren't waiting for you to interact—they're *already* talking about you. Companies that engage their audiences can build positive relationships, create a reservoir of goodwill to tap into when a crisis strikes, and help prevent false rumors from spreading before they take deep root.

If you work for a company, your social networks offer you free market research that used to cost many thousands of dollars. If you work for an advocacy group, your networks tell you which appeals are most likely to spur donations *before* you invest in a major campaign. If you work for a government agency, your social networks will let you know what public misperceptions you need to clear up.

Journalists are also turning to social media in droves to learn more about you. If you're not managing your reputation where your audiences are, you're nowhere—or worse.

SOCIAL MEDIA BY THE NUMBERS

- In September 2012, Twitter users in the United States visited the site more than 51 million times per week.

- In June 2012, Facebook averaged more than 550 million users every day.

- As of May 2012, 800 million unique users worldwide visited YouTube each month.

- LinkedIn members conducted an estimated 5.3 billion searches on the platform in 2012.

Sources: Burson-Marstellar, Experian, LinkedIn

72 SOCIAL MEDIA: SIX BEST PRACTICES

Many businesses, nonprofit organizations, and politicians operate their own "newsrooms" today by releasing official news through their social media networks.

Musicians tout new albums on their Twitter feeds. Businesses introduce new products on their Facebook pages. Presidential contenders announce their candidacies through YouTube videos.

News released via social media often makes its way into the mainstream press. It's still a bit strange for us "old school" journalists to see today's news anchors reporting on what some politician said on Twitter, but they do. Traditional journalists often base their reporting on a statement released through a company's (or individual's) social media account.

Therefore, you should treat social media as a nonstop media interview. Instead of fielding questions from professional journalists, you will participate in a conversation with customers, critics, and activists. But journalists will be watching what you say, so remember that your interactions with the online community can become newsworthy—and often do.

Here are six best practices to keep in mind when communicating through social media:

1. **Know the culture:** Every social media network has its own culture. It would be inappropriate to post a long business letter to Facebook, for example, but it might be okay to post a *link* to that letter. Spend some time getting to know each network before jumping in.

2. **Listen:** When starting with a new social media platform, listen to what people are saying about you. Are they criticizing your response to a crisis, praising your work, or expressing confusion with an old product's new feature? Listening before

talking will help you align your communications with your audience's needs.

3. **Participate:** This isn't a one-way press release but a two-way conversation. Engage with your audiences. It's okay to use your networks to promote your products, but don't make selling the only thing you do. Answer customers' questions, express gratitude for praise, and candidly admit imperfection.

4. **Use a more causal tone:** Most social networking sites are more casual than other forms of business communication. Casual doesn't mean racy, unnecessarily provocative, or unprofessional—it means that you come across as a "real" person, not a corporate lackey. One way to do that is to use everyday language instead of the formal business prose typically found in annual reports.

5. **Respond to negative feedback:** Many of our clients ask whether they should respond to negative feedback. The answer is usually yes. According to a 2011 Harris Interactive study, unhappy customers quickly forgave companies that responded to them. Thirty-three percent of customers who left a negative review on a shopping website ended up posting a *positive* review after receiving a response, while another 34 percent deleted the original review. Be cordial in your response—the rest of the audience will judge you based on the tone of your reply.

6. **Monitor:** Track your social media sites at least daily, if not hourly (or appoint someone who can). Little will make your company appear less interested in your audience than being absent from your own coverage. I'm regularly surprised by companies that fail to respond to scathing comments on their own social networks, leaving other customers to conclude that the original accusations are probably correct.

73 SOCIAL MEDIA: YOU'RE ALWAYS "ON THE RECORD"

The number one question I hear from executives about social media might surprise you. They want to know how they can prevent employees from secretly recording their staff meetings and uploading the audio or video to YouTube.

Many companies have social media policies aimed at preventing that type of behavior, and many of those policies have teeth, making unauthorized employee communications a fireable offense.

But the truth is that you can't prevent disgruntled employees from furtively recording you. Tens of millions of smartphones have mini audio recorders or video cameras, and you're powerless to stop an employee (or anyone else) from recording you without your knowledge and uploading the file to an anonymous social media account.

THEREFORE, THE USUAL MEDIA TRAINING ADVICE APPLIES: IF YOU DON'T WANT IT IN PRINT, DON'T SAY IT AT ALL.

Treat all of your public communications as if you're speaking at a press conference. You are. In an age when every employee, colleague, and partner can instantly become a reporter through their social media accounts, you need to remain more wary than ever of saying *anything* that could be used against you in the court of public opinion. That doesn't mean you can't communicate tough truths, but rather that you do so in a manner you wouldn't mind seeing splashed all over the web within minutes.

The same goes for *any* public communications. I'm constantly amazed by what I observe in public: attorneys sitting on packed Amtrak cars discussing sensitive cases loudly on their cell phones, business professionals working on documents marked "confidential" in plain sight on airplanes, and politicos hashing out controversial strategy over a Washington "power lunch" within earshot of fellow diners.

Those people have no idea who I am. I could be their opposing counsel, their direct business competitor, or a political reporter. And if I can use the information I learn against them, I will.

CASE STUDY: THE STORY OF "ACELA BOB"

On February 18, 2009, a lawyer named Bob Robbins rode Amtrak's 2 p.m. Acela train from Washington, DC to New York City.

While on the train, Mr. Robbins—head of the corporate and securities practice for the law firm Pillsbury Winthrop Shaw Pittman—phoned a colleague. The two men discussed their firm's plan to lay off 15 to 20 attorneys within a month. Mr. Robbins made a point of telling his colleague that the news was sensitive and must remain secret.

Unfortunately for Mr. Robbins, he said all of that rather loudly. Many of his fellow riders overheard the conversation, including one law student seated nearby who decided to email the "secret" news to the popular legal blog *Above the Law*.

The blog ran the story the next morning. Within hours, Pillsbury had little choice but to confirm the layoffs, writing: "We will be implementing reductions...we apologize for the unfortunate manner in which our deliberations about reductions have become public."

As a result of one loud cell phone call, Mr. Robbins's colleagues learned about the impending layoffs through a blog post, and his firm was forced to release the news one month ahead of schedule. Mr. Robbins's indiscreet phone call earned him a new nickname: Acela Bob.

74 SOCIAL MEDIA: ONCE YOU SAY IT, IT'S OUT THERE FOREVER

In 2011, New York Congressman Anthony Weiner resigned after accidentally tweeting a photo of himself in his underwear to his entire Twitter network (he meant to send the photo to just one person).

His was an extreme case. But he's far from alone in suffering negative consequences that resulted from the careless use of social media:

- James Andrews, a vice president with the PR firm Ketchum, tweeted, "I would die if I had to live here!" after landing in Memphis in 2009. Someone at Federal Express, his client in Memphis, saw the tweet. Andrews left Ketchum shortly afterward.

- GoDaddy.com CEO Bob Parsons lost thousands of customers in 2011 after uploading a YouTube video of himself killing an elephant during an African vacation.

- CNN pundit Roland Martin was suspended from the network in 2012 after tweeting a comment perceived as homophobic.

- Two top athletes—a Swiss soccer player and a Greek triple jumper—were kicked off their teams during the 2012 Olympic Summer Games for tweeting racist comments.

I expect you won't commit any gaffes as extreme as these. But you would be wise to remember one rule of the Internet age:

ONCE IT'S OUT THERE, IT'S OUT THERE FOREVER.

Your operating philosophy in the online world (as in the offline world) should be this: "How will this look if a stranger—or one of my critics—sees this and wants to start trouble?"

It's also worth mentioning the confusion some people have regarding the distinction between their personal and professional accounts.

Many social media users wrongly assume that they can write anything they want on their personal pages as long as they have a disclaimer in their profile that reads, "The views expressed here do not represent those of my employer."

Nonsense!

For practical purposes, there is *no difference* between your personal accounts and your professional ones. If the words, photos, and videos you post to your personal accounts reflect badly on you or your employer, you may find yourself suddenly embroiled in a major corporate crisis—or out of work.

And that assumes you got the job in the first place. The majority of hiring managers—some studies suggest more than 80 percent—look at a prospective employee's social media accounts before making a final hiring decision. An objectionable post can be all it takes to eliminate a job candidate.

It's okay to have personal and professional accounts with different content on each. It's usually fine to use personal networks to post family photos, root for our favorite sports teams, or offer a negative review about a Hollywood movie. But always steer clear of crass references to sex, gender, race, religion, or sexual orientation—and think carefully before posting controversial views that could come back to haunt you.

You should consider tightening your personal networks' privacy settings and restricting them to friends and family only. Restricting personal networks is more appropriate for some social networks than others—and even strict privacy settings don't guarantee total protection.

Therefore, the best advice is also the simplest: before hitting "send" on any post, pause and review it one final time.

75 BLOGS AND BLOGGERS

A "blog" can be many things. Strictly speaking, a blog is defined as an online web log with posts that appear in reverse chronological order. But given the broad range of blogs in the "blogosphere," that definition isn't particularly helpful.

Some blogs appear as polished online newspapers, while others consist of little more than incoherent rants. Some operate with the same professional standards of a well-run newsroom, while others spread baseless gossip and innuendo. Some have access to top government and business executives, are read by world leaders, and have larger audiences than many traditional newspapers and television networks. Others have little impact and few readers outside of immediate family and friends.

Altogether, there were more than 181 million blogs worldwide by the end of 2011, according to NM Incite, a social media research company. Although no one-size-fits-all advice can apply to *every* blog, these five rules of thumb may help:

1. **Do your homework:** Before agreeing to an interview with a blogger, visit the blog to get a sense of the blog's standards and the blogger's tone.

    If the blog appears to use objective journalistic standards, you can treat the interview the same as any other described in this book. If the blog or blogger relies more heavily on opinion and analysis, read several stories to help determine the site's ideological leanings or biases. Is the site liberal or conservative? Is the tone respectful or dismissive of differing opinions? Knowing a blog's viewpoint may help you anticipate the blogger's questions and shape your argument in advance.

2. **Decide whether to agree to an interview:** Although I generally advise spokespersons to accept interviews for stories in

which they'll be mentioned, there are exceptions to that rule. Here's one: If the blog or blogger has little regard for fairness and accuracy or represents a fringe view, you might pass. You may also have to turn down (or delay) interviews for logistical reasons. For example, if you're barraged with press calls during a crisis or have a small communications staff, you might have to prioritize larger news organizations and blogs over smaller ones.

3. **But...don't blow off smaller blogs:** Some blogs have small audiences but are quite influential and rank high on search engines. Don't let a blog's small readership be the sole determinant of whether you agree to an interview, especially if it reaches one of your core audiences. And even "unimportant" smaller blogs that don't reach a key audience can represent a good opportunity to practice your interviewing skills.

4. **Communicate in writing:** Many interviews with bloggers occur over email. That's especially helpful if you're unsure of the blogger's commitment to accuracy, since it allows you to maintain a paper trail. But don't be afraid of picking up the phone or meeting a blogger in person, particularly if the author appears to be fair.

5. **Consider participating in the comments section:** If the blogger gets a key fact wrong or misrepresents your views, consider posting a response in the comments section. Before jumping in, review what other commenters are saying and assess whether your comment is more likely to be perceived as helpful or inflammatory. If you leave a comment, be transparent about who you are and whom you work for.

76 ONLINE VIDEO, PODCASTS, AND SKYPE

It seems as if online video, podcasts, and Skype have been around forever, but it was only 2006 when YouTube took off and Skype introduced video calling.

These newer forms of communications are accessible to hundreds of millions of people for free, and many spokespersons are using the platforms to speak directly to their audiences, which often include journalists.

ONLINE VIDEO AND PODCASTS

A 2012 study conducted by the PR firm Burson-Marstellar found that more than 4 billion videos are viewed *every day* on YouTube. The study also found that a whopping 72 hours of video are uploaded by users to the video-sharing site *every minute.*

Podcasts, which are similar to online video, have also gained popularity. The key difference is that instead of being viewed online, podcasts are typically downloaded from the Internet to a personal device, such as an MP3 player.

When shooting online videos or podcasts, media spokespersons most commonly speak directly into the camera. Visualize a specific person in your audience and speak directly to him or her, just as you would if you were having a chat at a local coffee shop.

Online videos and podcasts are more intimate than television interviews. Therefore, your tone should be even *more* conversational, focused on making a personal connection with one viewer at a time. Add a fair dose of personal warmth—unless you're speaking about a tragic topic, you'll almost always fare better by appearing more relatable.

SKYPE

Skype is a software application that allows its users to make free video calls over the Internet. As of August 2012, Skype had 254 million monthly active users, according to company CEO Tony Bates.

Many news programs use Skype (or similar technologies) to interview spokespersons. Doing so makes sense for cash-strapped news organizations—instead of sending a camera crew to your home or office at great expense, they can save money by asking you to remain at your desk and conduct the interview via Skype. In addition to saving money, Skype can help save time on breaking news stories (news organizations can put you on the air *now* instead of waiting for you to drive to the studio) and bridge insurmountable geographical distances.

Skype offers some obvious advantages, but it also requires you to focus on a few additional points:

1. **Limit your movements:** Depending on your computer's bandwidth, you might look "jumpy." Whereas television has 30 frames per second, which the eye reads as constant movement, a slow Internet connection only has 10—15, which the eye reads as separate frames. Therefore, limit your head, hand, and arm movements unless you have a good camera and fast connection. Skype is the only format in which gesturing can *hurt* your performance.

2. **Buy a headset and/or webcam:** These are important investments if you're likely to be doing such interviews. Don't settle for the cheapest options; quality matters.

3. **Set up your shot:** Simplify the background by removing small items, and adjust overhead lights and floor and desk lamps to add brightness to the frame and reduce shadows.

77 FIVE ADDITIONAL MEDIA FORMATS

Spokespersons may encounter a few additional media formats. Be sure to familiarize yourself with these five possibilities:

1. **Editorial-Board Meetings:** Many newspapers have editorial boards, which are composed of a small group of editors who write the editorials, or "official viewpoints," that appear in each morning's paper. The editors who pen them are typically not news reporters (whose reporting is supposed to avoid expressing personal viewpoints). Editorials are different than "op-eds," which are usually written by members of the community.

   Meetings with editorial boards are opportunities to influence the editors to adopt your viewpoint. Treat these meetings the same way you would a news interview: anything you say can be quoted, and some editorial board meetings may be audio- and/or videotaped. Some editors ask aggressive questions, especially of spokespersons who represent a controversial brand or idea, so prepare thoroughly for your meeting.

2. **Deskside Briefings:** Deskside briefings are similar to meetings with editorial boards, but are usually one-on-one exchanges with an individual journalist at his or her office (hence the name "deskside") rather than with larger groups. The casual and often friendly nature of deskside briefings can lead spokespersons to stray off their messages, so remember to treat everything you say as a quotable comment.

3. **Walk and Talks:** Have you ever seen a television interviewer conduct an interview while walking down a street or hallway with the interviewee? Some reporters are fond of conducting interviews as "walk and talks," since they tend to relax the person being interviewed and are more visually interesting than a typical in-studio interview.

This can be a difficult format, since you have to focus on where you're walking in addition to relaying your message. Walk slowly—and if you find yourself getting distracted, stop walking for a moment and turn toward the interviewer while making a key point.

4. **Demos:** Some talk shows, including daytime chat programs, ask guests to do a demonstration, or "demo." Chefs show viewers how to cook lasagna, home decorators demonstrate how to inexpensively design a living room, and physicians teach people how to perform a self-examination.

    Delivering a demo in just a few short minutes can be a major challenge. Do several on-camera practice rounds in advance to get your timing and delivery down, and be prepared to handle any unexpected moments that occur.

5. **Comedy Shows:** One thing I've learned through the years is that almost everyone thinks they're funny. So when they appear on a late-night talk show such as *The Tonight Show* or *The Daily Show with Jon Stewart*, their inclination is to try to crack a joke or two. It's usually a bad idea.

    Unless you're a comedian, it's usually best to avoid competing for punch lines. Stephen Colbert, host of Comedy Central's *The Colbert Report*, even tells his guests beforehand to play it straight. Let the comedian do the jokes—comedy isn't as easy as it looks. Just bring your good humor, a warm smile, and a willingness to go along with the joke.

Crisis Communications: The 10 Truths Of A Crisis

"When written in Chinese, the word 'crisis' is composed of two characters—one represents danger, and the other represents opportunity."

John F. Kennedy

78 WHAT IS A CRISIS?

In this section, you will learn 10 truths that usually determine the outcome of a corporate or personal crisis.

First, though, it's worth defining the term *crisis*. A crisis is an event, precipitated by a specific incident, that attracts critical media attention and lasts for a definite period of time.

A crisis may be different than ordinary bad press. For example, a government agency that announces an unpopular new fee may get some negative press, but will probably not face a full-fledged crisis. But if that government agency is forced to raise fees due to financial mismanagement, it probably will.

Crises can be classified into eight categories, some of which may overlap, depending on the situation:

1. **Natural Disasters:** Weather-related events, such as hurricanes, tornadoes, fires, floods, or droughts

2. **Unnatural Disasters:** Intentional or unintentional incidents, such as industrial accidents, plane crashes, workplace violence, or terrorist attacks

3. **Product Crises:** Defective or dangerous products, product recalls

4. **Policy Crises:** Unpopular or controversial policy positions; changes to policies, procedures, or fees

5. **Process Crises:** Failure to deliver promised goods, incompetent customer service, slow order fulfillment

6. **Employee Crises:** Layoffs, sexual harassment or discrimination, illegal labor practices

7. **Personal Crises:** Sexual affairs, personal conflicts of interest, questionable behavior or decision-making

8. **Wrongdoing:** Violations of law, such as embezzlement or fraudulent financial reporting

These eight categories highlight an important point: the vast majority of crises are predictable, meaning they can (and should) be planned for in advance. Whereas the number of *things* that can go wrong within any company is virtually limitless, the number of *types* of things that can go wrong is limited.

If you've never done a risk assessment, you can begin by listing the five crises that are a combination of the most likely to occur and the most potentially damaging to your reputation. (You'll learn more about how to prepare for a crisis in lesson 90.)

As examples, here are a few potential crises that some of our clients have identified as their most likely crisis scenarios:

- One trucking company prepared for the possibility of one of its drivers colliding with a school bus while intoxicated.

- One medical testing company prepared for the possibility of a severe snowfall preventing it from shipping time-sensitive patient tests to their labs before their expiration dates.

- A privately held utility company anticipated that its president's salary would attract the scrutiny of the media and the ire of the public after announcing a double-digit rate hike.

- A government agency predicted that the public would be outraged over a controversial (but necessary) rule change affecting international travelers.

79 TRUTH ONE: YOU'RE GOING TO SUFFER—AT LEAST AT FIRST

Legendary investor Warren Buffett once said, "It takes 20 years to build a reputation and five minutes to ruin it."

I'd add one line to his quote: a crisis itself doesn't always do the most damage – the *handling* of it often does.

That's already evident to you, as you've surely noticed that some crises seem to have a short shelf life while others linger for months, taking down top executives, destroying share price, and shattering a once-respected brand's image.

A well-handled crisis, on the other hand, can be an opportunity for a brand to demonstrate its competence and enhance its image. Several years ago, an Oxford University study called *The Impact of Catastrophes on Shareholder Value* found that companies that managed a crisis well actually *gained* value just two months after a catastrophe.

Authors Rory F. Knight and Deborah J. Pretty explain:

> *"Why would some catastrophes lead to an increase in shareholder value? One explanation from our research is that there are two elements to the catastrophic impact. The first is the immediate estimate of the associated economic loss. The second hinges on management's ability to deal with the aftermath. Although all catastrophes have an initial negative impact on value, paradoxically they offer an opportunity for management to demonstrate their talent in dealing with difficult circumstances."*

Their study concluded that companies in crisis will suffer—at least at first—but that companies that handle a crisis successfully can avoid incurring irrevocable, long-term damage.

Take the tale of two car companies. When Saturn (now defunct) had to recall some of its defective automobiles, it offered its inconvenienced customers a free car wash and barbecue meal while they waited for their cars to be repaired. Toyota, on the other hand, suffered months of bad press over reports of cars accelerating without warning before finally—and reluctantly— recalling millions of cars due to those widespread concerns.

You can guess which response played better with journalists and the public.

THE FOUR STAGES OF A CRISIS

Jane Jordan-Meier, author of *The Four Stages of Highly Effective Crisis Management*, argues that there are four predictable stages in most crises:

Stage One: The breaking news, "what happened?" stage.

Stage Two: The make it or break it, reputation-forming stage, during which the media focuses on victims and the response.

Stage Three: The finger-pointing stage. By doing everything right in stage two, companies can minimize the length and severity of this stage.

Step Four: The fallout/resolution stage. This stage marks the end of the crisis; there is some resolution. There might be a funeral, a government inquiry, or a Senate hearing.

In many instances, companies have the power to contain crises and prevent them from becoming larger indictments of their brands. Like many companies in crisis, Toyota allowed a crisis about something specific (a defective product) to become a referendum on its very competence. It allowed the crisis to jump the "fire line" from a limited crisis to one that damaged its overall reputation. Saturn, on the other hand, successfully contained its crisis and prevented it from jumping the fire line.

80 TRUTH TWO: YOU'LL BE CAST AS A GOOD GUY OR A BAD GUY

"There are only two or three human stories, and they go on repeating themselves as fiercely as if they had never happened before." – Willa Cather, author

When a crisis strikes, the media cast roles almost immediately.

News organizations typically bestow only two starring roles: the good guy and the bad guy. That's because most media stories strip the narrative down to its most basic parts, resulting in each character being presented as an incomplete figure.

The actions you take in the earliest moments of a crisis will help determine how the media cast your role. If your response is tone-perfect from the start, you stand a greater chance of being perceived as the good guy—or at least *not* the bad guy. The media want to know that you "get it"—that you fully grasp the accusations being leveled against you, understand the scope of the problem, and have the ability to effectively manage the crisis.

But if something about your tone is off—if you come across as defensive, dismissive, or uncompassionate—the media will portray you as the bad guy. And once the media cast you in that role, you're going to find it difficult to convince them you deserve to be recast as a more heroic character.

As discouraging as that might sound, consider these two pieces of good news:

1. **Most crises are (at least somewhat) predictable:** That means you can plan and practice your response to a crisis long before it ever occurs. (You will learn more about preparing for a crisis in lesson 90.)

2. **The media's methods of reporting crises are *also* predictable:** That means you can anticipate, within a reasonable degree of certainty, how the media would evaluate your handling of the crisis.

CASE STUDY: JET BLUE GETS GROUNDED

In February 2007, Jet Blue flights were grounded at a New York City airport after a snowstorm hit the area. One packed plane sat on the runway for 11 hours without sufficient food or water. Passengers could see the gate just yards away but weren't allowed to exit. Furious customers uploaded YouTube videos documenting smelly toilets and stifling heat, creating a PR nightmare for the airline.

CEO David Neeleman gave several interviews in the days that followed, offering profuse apologies to the affected passengers. Even better, he quickly issued a "Passenger Bill of Rights," guaranteeing compensation to anyone experiencing similar problems in the future (it also applied retroactively). Mr. Neeleman was seen by the media as a "good guy" who got it. News coverage even turned positive, praising his handling of the crisis. As a result, the crisis had little long-term impact on the airline.

In addition to your initial response to a crisis, one additional factor determines how you will be cast in a crisis: who you are. The media love a good David and Goliath story. If you're the "little guy" fighting entrenched power despite the long odds against you, you'll probably be cast as the heroic David.

But if you work for a giant company, bureaucratic government agency, or multinational bank, you're likelier to be labeled an unfeeling Goliath. Don't despair in this event—even big institutions often succeed in media crises. But they need to do everything right from the start to avoid being cast as a bad guy.

81 TRUTH THREE: YOU MUST COMMUNICATE IMMEDIATELY

When a crisis strikes and reporters are knocking at your door, you should begin communicating immediately. Often, that means making a public statement within the hour. You should be "present in your own coverage," which will help establish your company as the primary source of information for reporters.

If you don't talk, others will. Reporters have to file their stories with or without your cooperation, and they'll have no choice but to fill a void of information by getting their intelligence from an external source—a former employee who doesn't have her facts straight, a critic who's been warning of this looming disaster for years, or a competitor who secretly relishes your misfortune.

It's no surprise that those outside sources are often inaccurate— but if you're not present in your own coverage, those false charges can (and often do) become widely accepted "facts."

That dynamic is truer than ever in the age of Twitter, when anyone with a smartphone can tweet a false allegation to thousands of people in one nanosecond with a click of a button. If you're not present in your own coverage, you've voluntarily surrendered a critical opportunity to rebut false charges and disseminate accurate information.

There's another important reason to begin communicating immediately: reporters tend to provide more sympathetic coverage to sources who talk. The *lack* of a public response, on the other hand, usually comes across to the media and the public as a sign of guilt. Fairly or not, we're inclined to believe people who show up and speak, and tend to assume the worst when people refuse to emerge from the safety of their offices. Communicating early conveys openness and a genuine desire to solve the problem. Clamming up suggests the opposite.

CASE STUDY: THE EXXON VALDEZ OIL SPILL

One of the most infamous examples of an inept crisis response occurred in 1989, when the Exxon *Valdez* oil tanker ran aground in Alaska's Prince William Sound. The massive ship dumped more than 11 million gallons of crude oil into U.S. waters, the worst spill ever in the States at that time.

The spill itself was bad enough, but Exxon CEO Lawrence Rawl compounded his company's troubles by failing to be present in his own coverage. He refused to make a media statement for almost a week. Even worse, he waited three weeks before visiting the accident site.

Mr. Rawl's failure to personally respond more quickly led the media to conclude that he didn't take the crisis seriously enough and wasn't fully committed to solving the problem. More than two decades later, Exxon is still viewed by many as a villainous corporate wrongdoer.

You will rarely have all of the facts early in a crisis. Don't let that prevent you from communicating quickly. You can begin with a statement that conveys your awareness of the incident, your investigation of it, and your plan to update the press as soon as you know more. Here's an example:

> "At approximately 4:05 p.m. central daylight time, a large tank exploded at our facility. The fire department is on the scene and the fire is still burning. Unfortunately, some of our employees were injured, and a few of our people are being transported to a local hospital. We do not know how many people are injured or the extent of their injuries. Nothing is more important to us than the well-being of our staff, and we are doing everything possible to make sure they receive the care they need. I will update you again as soon as I know more, hopefully within an hour."

82 TRUTH FOUR: THE MEDIA WILL SIDE WITH THE VICTIMS

When the media cast roles after a crisis strikes, no voice is more compelling than that of the victim's (or, when a company is accused of something it didn't do, the *perceived* victim).

Consider these examples:

- When Toyota was accused of making vehicles that automatically accelerated to terrifying speeds without warning, the most compelling stories came from drivers who feared for their family's lives.

- When banks were vilified for giving unfair subprime mortgage loans to homeowners, the most dramatic narratives came from ordinary Americans who were struggling to pay off their massive debt.

- When the U.S. government was accused of an inept crisis response in New Orleans following 2005's Hurricane Katrina, the most sympathetic voices belonged to the survivors who had lost family members, their homes, or their livelihoods.

People who have been injured by another party, especially by a larger institution, are inherently relatable. That's particularly true when the victims are "ordinary" people, since we tend to put ourselves in their shoes when we read, hear, or watch their stories.

As you might imagine, it's challenging for companies to appear as sympathetic as an individual victim. But it's not impossible. The best way to earn goodwill with the audience is to treat the victims with genuine humanity in your response.

THE PUBLIC WILL BASE MUCH OF ITS OPINION OF YOU ON THE WAY YOU TREAT THE VICTIMS (OR PERCEIVED VICTIMS) DURING A CRISIS.

That may sound obvious, but organizations in crisis tend to over-rely on the facts, especially if the facts prove their innocence. They forget that facts alone are rarely enough in a crisis. If their facts are right but their tone is wrong, the public is probably going to view them as clueless, heartless, or both.

CASE STUDY: A HOSPITAL'S RESPONSE FAILS TO FOCUS ON VICTIMS

Daniel Blejer, a Virginia scientist, died in 2005 of Creutzfeldt-Jakob disease (CJD), a rapidly moving neurological disorder that can cause dementia in weeks or months. He may have contracted the disease when surgical forceps used during an unrelated procedure weren't sufficiently sterilized. According to *The Washington Post*, "Sterilization methods do not always eradicate the infectious agent from surgical instruments exposed to CJD because it is not a conventional bacteria or virus."

The Post spoke to the chairman of neurological surgery for Seattle's Harborview Medical Center, which had exposed up to 12 patients (not Mr. Blejer) to a similar disease. When asked why the hospital didn't use new forceps instead of sterilizing them, he pointed out that new forceps cost $800 each, and said:

"That's a lot of money. There's a cost-benefit ratio."

The doctor appeared to be saying that the safety of his patients wasn't worth an $800 investment. That cold response was unnecessary, especially because the hospital had changed its policies and pledged to use each instrument only once in the future.

A more victim-focused response might have said:

"Nothing is more important to us than the safety of our patients. That's why we've changed our policy and will only use these instruments once from now on. Our patients deserve nothing less."

83 TRUTH FIVE: THE SPOKESPERSON YOU CHOOSE SPEAKS VOLUMES

Although this book focuses on teaching *you* how to become a better spokesperson, there may be circumstances when you should select someone else to communicate during a crisis. That's because the person who you choose to communicate during a crisis tells the public a lot about your handling of it.

If you select someone too high on the corporate hierarchy chart, the public will conclude that the crisis is bigger than it originally thought. If you select someone too low, the public will conclude that you're not taking the crisis seriously enough. When forced with a similar decision, I generally advise clients to err on the side of going too high rather than too low.

That doesn't necessarily mean starting with the CEO. Matt Eventoff, a New Jersey based public speaking coach, smartly advises his clients *not* to start with the top leader; that way, the CEO can step in if the initial spokesperson blows the response. If you begin with the CEO and he or she mangles the response, Eventoff says, you have nowhere "up" to go, and will be forced to choose a spokesperson lower on the hierarchy chart.

That's sound logic for most crises, but giant, reputation-defining events—massive oil spills, incidents with mass casualties, political scandals—may still demand the CEO as spokesperson from the start. The size and scope of a crisis will help you determine the right spokesperson; generally speaking, the bigger the crisis, the more senior the spokesperson.

Jane Jordan-Meier, author of *The Four Stages of Highly Effective Crisis Management*, recommends a two-pronged approach to some larger crises that pairs an executive with a technical expert:

> *"Even though the CEO may know less about the details, his or her physical presence sends two powerful messages: 'I care*

and I am accountable.' The head of operations and/or the key technical staff must also be there to deal with the detail."

That "multiple spokesperson" approach offers another advantage: it allows you to strategically deploy different spokespersons to handle different mediums. You might use a knowledgeable but uncharismatic technical expert to handle print interviews, and a less knowledgeable but more charismatic leader to handle broadcast interviews.

In addition to using the hierarchy chart as a guide for selecting the right spokesperson, you should choose a person capable of delivering your messages with the compassion and care that a crisis demands. Ms. Jordan-Meier uses a test she calls the "head/heart principle" to help pick the right spokesperson. The right spokesperson, she says, must avoid the cognitive dissonance that occurs when a representative delivers the right words in the wrong way. Spokespersons should be capable of bringing the head and the heart together, and "must be totally believable when they are expressing concern."

In his book *Damage Control*, crisis communications pro Eric Dezenhall argues that too many companies underestimate the importance of selecting the right spokesperson:

> *"Most corporations under siege devote far too much attention to strategy and not enough on the key personalities…If given a choice between a thorough plan and a good leader, go with the leader, because people rarely separate the event from the personalities that dominate the event."*

Finally, it's important to note that for crises of limited duration at a specific site, the media may never want to speak to an executive. In those cases, reporters often prefer to talk to people on the ground. If an explosion occurs at your Wyoming plant, the media will likely want to speak with the manager of that facility, not an executive from your Denver headquarters.

84 TRUTH SIX: YOUR RECEPTIONIST NEEDS MEDIA TRAINING

I once wrote an article for the Mr. Media Training Blog to help executives prepare for an unexpected crisis; it included the following suggestion:

> "If a journalist calls you and asks you for comment about a breaking crisis that you haven't heard about yet, you don't have to comment immediately. Tell the reporter it's the first you've heard about it, that you'll look into it immediately, and that you'll return their phone call as soon as you know more."

I thought that was sound advice, but a journalist wrote in to take me to task. She wrote this pointed response:

> "Who cares if executives turn down an interview? I regularly circumvent the executives at the beginning of a crisis. I prefer to start talking to the receptionist instead. He or she always knows more anyway—and they're usually more willing to talk."

That's a good point. Reporters occasionally avoid "official" channels in an effort to get more candid, less scripted responses from staffers lower on the hierarchy chart. And too often, receptionists—notoriously more plugged in to company gossip than most are—inadvertently say something to reporters that they shouldn't.

It's always a good idea to train your receptionists how to handle media calls, but it's even more critical to prepare them for an unexpected crisis.

Receptionists are your frontline personnel. They're frequently the first people to learn of a crisis, tipped off by a phone call from a reporter, a colleague, or a stranger. There's little point in investing thousands of dollars to train your executive team how to manage a crisis effectively if your receptionists or administrative assistants undermine your best efforts by saying something they shouldn't.

And it's not just receptionists. You should also prepare security guards, who may be the first people to greet uninvited camera crews. If security guards aren't told otherwise, their first instinct too often is to place a hand in front of the camera's lens while impolitely telling the cameraperson to get lost. That aggressive footage usually gets aired.

Don't overlook the spouses of your executives, either. They may answer their home phones during a burgeoning crisis and say something like, "Yeah, I think there was an explosion or something at the plant. But you just missed Dawn—she already headed down there."

Oops. Dawn's husband just became the reporter's confirming source.

You don't have to enroll your receptionists, security guards, and other support personnel in a media training class. Instead, create a policy that describes the protocol for unexpected contacts with the media. Share it with your entire staff. Don't just do it once—they'll need regular reminders.

And remember: When you have temps staffing your phones along the way, fill them in on your media procedures. Those "temps" have your company's reputation in their hands.

85   TRUTH SEVEN: BURYING BAD PARTS OF THE STORY MAKES IT WORSE

In the earliest moments of a breaking crisis, journalists rarely know all of the facts. They may have discovered only a small sliver of the story, leading executives to conclude they should deal solely with the parts of the story the media already know about rather than revealing additional—and more damning—parts of the story.

Their rationale usually boils down to "Why make a difficult situation even worse?" But that kind of short-term thinking often backfires, activating the media's "gotcha" instinct and worsening the tone of your coverage.

If you allow reporters to discover each new part of the story on their own—with each revelation spawning its own story—you will keep the crisis alive longer than necessary. That steady drip, drip, drip of new information will diminish your credibility that much more—assuming you still have any left at all.

As difficult as it may be to get all of the facts out at the very beginning of a crisis, it's usually the right decision. Don't peel the Band-Aid back bit by bit. Tear it off quickly. You may still be accused of causing the crisis or exercising terrible judgment (perhaps you're guilty on both counts), but you'll usually reduce the damage by dealing with the crisis forthrightly.

It's true that you may not know all of the facts at first. In that case, it's imperative that you tell reporters you don't have all of the facts yet, are working hard to obtain them, and will share them as soon as you learn more. You might even tell them when they can expect the next statement from you, which will include any new information you learn.

If you don't know all of the facts, don't bluff. If you're asked how many of your hotel's guests have been illegally videotaped by a spy camera placed in a bathroom air vent by a rogue employee, it's probably a bad idea to say, "Not many—there was only a camera in one room," unless you're certain. It's better to say, "We don't know yet. We're only aware of a camera in one room, but we're checking every guest room to make sure."

CASE STUDY: SUSAN G. KOMEN FOR THE CURE

Susan G. Komen for the Cure, the world's largest breast cancer nonprofit organization, suffered a major blow to its once-sterling reputation in 2012.

In December 2011, Komen decided to stop giving grants to Planned Parenthood, a women's health provider that offers abortion services. Komen knew its decision would be controversial and tried to keep it quiet. But two months later, Planned Parenthood told its supporters about Komen's decision. The news spread quickly, outraging thousands of Komen's donors who also supported Planned Parenthood.

Komen founder Nancy Brinker insisted that her group's decision wasn't politically motivated. When asked whether newly hired executive Karen Handel—a former political candidate who had previously spoken out against Planned Parenthood—had anything to do with the decision, Ms. Brinker said, "Karen did not have anything to do with this decision." But after resigning days later, Ms. Handel admitted, "I openly acknowledge my role in the matter."

Internal memos soon leaked out which suggested that Komen had intentionally created rules that would apply to only one of the 2,000 organizations to which it gave grants, Planned Parenthood, and that it did so for political reasons.

The group's fundraising took a major hit, with fewer women participating in Komen's annual races. In Washington, DC, 40,000 women raced in 2011; only 26,000 did in 2012. Similar drops were reported in several other U.S. cities.

86 TRUTH EIGHT: SOCIAL MEDIA CAN MAKE OR BREAK YOU

Imagine you're the communications director for Hartown Manufacturing, a midsize company based in California. You're responsible for all communications in the western United States.

One morning, you arrive at work and log in to your Twitter account. You're scrolling through the rather dull tweets when you suddenly see one that takes your breath away: "Breaking News: Major Explosion at Salt Lake City Hartown Plant."

Within minutes, many people are tweeting about it, spreading rumors along the way. Some eyewitnesses claim they've seen ambulances pulling away with dozens of victims. One claims a plant supervisor has been killed. You call a colleague who works at the plant who tells you that no one knows whether anybody was badly hurt—and that no ambulances have arrived yet.

You immediately post that accurate information to Hartown's social media pages. Journalists who follow your feeds see your posts and decide against reporting any of the rumors they've read about possible injuries or deaths until you confirm them.

That type of scenario is commonplace in the age of social media, and it underscores three important truths:

1. The public and the press may learn of a crisis affecting your company through their social media networks before you even know there's a problem.

2. People will begin discussing (and speculating about) your crisis before you've had time to obtain the facts.

3. You need to use your social media channels to immediately correct misinformation and establish yourself as a primary source of accurate information.

Most reporters now use social media as an essential tool of crisis reporting. As Jane Jordan-Meier reported in *The Four Stages of Highly Effective Crisis Management,* "Two journalists I spoke with saw Twitter as the new police scanner." You can no longer afford to relegate social media to being of secondary importance.

Communicate through your social media networks as quickly as possible, ideally within half an hour of learning about an incident. You can include links to lengthier statements and additional resources in your posts.

There's one additional way to help manage a crisis using social media: be engaged with your social networks *before* a crisis strikes. You'll need fans to defend your integrity when something goes wrong, and few people are more credible than the unaffiliated third parties who voluntarily vouch for you.

CASE STUDY: DOMINO'S PIZZA AND A DISGUSTING VIDEO (V)

In 2009, an employee of a North Carolina Domino's franchise filmed a coworker sticking cheese up his nose before appearing to send the food out for delivery. The two workers uploaded the video to YouTube, where it quickly racked up a million views. Television anchors showed the disgusting clip on their newscasts and customers stopped ordering pizza.

Company president Patrick Doyle waited two days before finally responding. He issued a two-minute YouTube apology, in which he appeared genuinely pained by the incident. He was deservedly given credit by many crisis management professionals for releasing the heartfelt video— but most suggested that he waited too long and incurred unnecessary financial and reputational damage by waiting 48 hours.

Mr. Doyle's response was noteworthy for one additional reason: it was the first time a major company president used YouTube as the primary method of responding to a crisis.

87 TRUTH NINE: YOU NEED TO APOLOGIZE THE RIGHT WAY

Many executives are reluctant to issue a full and unequivocal apology after making a mistake. That's not because they're bad or uncaring people. More commonly, it's a human reaction from a defensive person who feels that his or her well-intentioned motives were misunderstood.

As a result, the executive usually issues a hedged "half apology" that goes something like this:

> *"If you were offended by what I said, then I am sorry."*

That type of "if/then" apology, which places the burden on the offended person rather than the offender, tends to inflame a crisis instead of ending it. The equivocation almost inevitably fails to satisfy the public, forcing the executive to issue a second, more complete apology several days later:

> *"I said something offensive, and I apologize. I listened carefully to your feedback and completely understand your reaction. I will learn from my mistake to make sure it doesn't happen again. I sincerely apologize."*

That's much better, but by waiting several days to issue that second apology, the executive will unnecessarily suffer additional damage *and* diminish the impact of their second apology. You're better off skipping the first apology entirely and beginning with the second one instead.

The best apologies offer no excuses and pledge specific action to ensure the mistake never happens again. That means you might have to sacrifice something, even if doing so is painful.

For example, I once worked with a public organization whose chief executive was accused of abusing his expense account. Although everything he did was technically legal, it looked to the public that he had abused the perks of his office (it looked that way to me as well). I advised that he would need to cut a personal check for tens (or hundreds) of thousands of dollars to reimburse the organization and apologize unequivocally for his error in judgment. He refused. He was soon dismissed from the organization, his reputation forever tarnished.

CASE STUDY: PENN STATE UNIVERSITY SEXUAL ABUSE SCANDAL

In 2011, Penn State University was at the center of a major crisis when former assistant football coach Jerry Sandusky was charged with sexually molesting at least eight boys over the previous two decades.

Top officials at the school were accused of failing to report the incident to police, and several people—including the school's president, and legendary football coach Joe Paterno—were fired.

The first statements released by university officials were self-serving and defensive. But the Board of Trustees quickly released this tone-perfect apology:

> "The Board of Trustees...is outraged by the horrifying details contained in the Grand Jury Report. As parents, alumni and members of the Penn State Community, our hearts go out to all of those impacted by these terrible events, especially the tragedies involving children and their families. We cannot begin to express the combination of sorrow and anger that we feel about the allegations surrounding Jerry Sandusky. We hear those of you who feel betrayed and we want to assure all of you that the Board will take swift, decisive action...The Board will appoint a Special Committee...to determine what failures occurred, who is responsible and what measures are necessary to insure that this never happens at our University again."

88 TRUTH TEN: YOUR LAWYERS CAN MAKE THE CRISIS WORSE

When a crisis strikes, many attorneys have the same instinct: to clamp down on corporate communications and make the fewest number of public statements possible (if any at all). That's because an attorney's primary job is to minimize future financial payouts and, in cases of criminal wrongdoing, to reduce your culpability.

But that's a narrow prism through which to view a crisis, and it may not be sufficient to keep your business afloat. Too often, attorneys fail to take your long-term reputation into account. They also neglect to consider the impact of a crisis on employee recruitment, retention, productivity, and morale, as well as customer, shareholder, and donor loyalty.

In some crises, the amount of damage to your reputation can *exceed* the legal payout. Sure, your lawyer's legal strategy may result in a courthouse victory three years from now, but it may come at the steep cost of years of unflattering headlines.

Crises require you to make tough choices, occasionally ones that pit sound legal advice against sound communications advice.

For example, I once asked a top executive in crisis whether her top goal was to keep her job (which would be accompanied by a drawn-out legal case and severe damage to her reputation) or to maintain her reputation in the long term, which would require her to leave her job (but allow her to ditch the legal case). Based on dozens of case studies and the predictable stages most crises follow, I counseled her that she would have to make a difficult choice: her job or her reputation.

She insisted she could keep both and failed to act. Within weeks, she lost her job—*and* her reputation.

When faced with such a choice, ask yourself the following three questions:

1. What's the right thing to do?

2. Have I received input from legal *and* communications professionals and given both perspectives consideration?

3. Can I develop a strategy that marries the best legal *and* PR advice? Better yet, can I find an attorney who excels in communications and fully supports the PR function?

INSURANCE COMPANIES

Like attorneys, insurance companies typically have the sole goal of reducing their payouts. Worse, many insurance policies actually *prohibit* you from doing the right thing. For example, my company's insurance policy reads:

> *"You must not admit liability for or settle or make or promise any payment in respect of any claim, loss or damage which may be covered under this Policy."*

In other words, if a crisis hits my firm and I determine that an admission of wrongdoing is the best way to minimize the crisis and keep my company out of the headlines, I can't offer one. Doing so might result in a voided claim and a canceled policy.

Still, this isn't always the case. Jonathan Bernstein, president of Bernstein Crisis Management, advises clients to find a company more enlightened in its approach to crisis communications. Speak to your carrier—some errors and omissions insurance contracts have a crisis-management component. If worst comes to worst, you could always cancel your policy and go it alone so long as the potential payout is low and the risk of inaction is high. That's a risky strategy, so consult a lawyer and insurance professional before going "bare."

89 WHAT TO DO WHEN YOU'RE NOT GUILTY

After beating charges of larceny and fraud in 1987, former U.S. Secretary of Labor Ray Donovan famously asked, "Which office do I go to get my reputation back?"

Although the media are often right, you probably don't need much convincing that they have convicted innocent people far too many times:

- After the 1996 Atlanta Olympics bombing that killed one person and injured more than 100, the media presented local security guard Richard Jewell as the likely culprit. He was innocent.

- Many outlets implied that California Rep. Gary Condit was involved in the death of intern Chandra Levy, who disappeared in Washington, DC in 2001. Although the two had a sexual relationship, Mr. Condit was innocent.

- In 2006, three male Duke University lacrosse players were accused of raping a female student at a house party. The media portrayed them as out-of-control, entitled athletes. They were innocent.

When the media have you in their sights, it can be difficult to mount a successful defense. But there are at least three tactics that can help you survive the glare of the media spotlight:

1. **Be "super" open:** The media tend to perceive those who talk as innocent and those who don't as guilty. When you're falsely accused, nothing is as disarming to a reporter as a spokesperson who eagerly shares information. Meet with the reporter. Go to his or her office. Your mere presence will force most reporters to reevaluate whether you're guilty as charged.

2. **Bring a lawyer:** Although hiding behind a wall of attorneys can be viewed as defensive, it may be your best option if a news organization is about to report an inaccurate story. Threatening a libel suit may make the news organization reconsider running the piece, particularly if you bring substantial evidence to convince them they're wrong.

3. **Offer your own proof:** In some cases, there is a place for harder-edged tactics. Crisis pro Eric Dezenhall argues that sometimes you have to "do the media's job for them." That means you might hire a private investigator to look into the background of any accusers or conduct a "parallel" investigation to uncover facts that your critics aren't finding—or are purposely ignoring.

CASE STUDY: TACO BELL AGGRESSIVELY REBUTS FALSE CHARGE

When an Alabama law firm filed a class-action lawsuit against Taco Bell in 2011 for allegedly using less than 50 percent ground beef in its beef filling, the fast-food giant responded aggressively.

The company took out a full-page ad that corrected the record in major newspapers. They claimed their tacos used 88 percent beef and 12 percent spices and other ingredients, and said they "plan to take legal action against those who have made false claims against our seasoned beef."

The law firm dropped its suit within three months, to which Taco Bell responded with another ad asking, "Would it kill you to say you're sorry? As for the lawyers who brought this suit: You got it wrong, and you're probably feeling pretty bad right about now. But you know what always helps? Saying to everyone, 'I'm sorry.'" Taco Bell's aggressive response isn't right for every company in crisis—but in their case, it was a brilliant strategy that effectively diminished the crisis.

90 HOW TO PREPARE FOR A CRISIS

"Once you hear the thunder, it's too late to build the ark." That old proverb, used for decades by crisis communicators, teaches that the single best way to "win" a crisis is by preparing for it well in advance.

This lesson will offer five steps you can take to prepare for a crisis, and the right way to conduct a "real-time" crisis drill.

1. **Assemble a "crisis" team:** A crisis team should include your top leadership as well as key representatives from each of your company's major departments, including operations, sales, legal, human resources, and finance.

2. **Brainstorm potential crises:** Turn to lesson 78, go one-by-one through the eight categories of crises, and brainstorm the possible crises that could befall your organization in each category.

3. **Reduce your list:** Cut down those ideas to the five crises that are a combination of the most damaging *and* the most likely to occur. You will likely need several meetings with your crisis team to brainstorm potential crises and reduce your list to the top five.

4. **Develop your response:** Schedule five two-hour meetings, one per month. For each meeting, select one of the crises and discuss how you would respond (as well as *who* would respond). After each meeting, write an action plan that details your response to that crisis and share it with the members of the team.

5. **Conduct crisis drills:** No matter how thoroughly you've developed your crisis response, there are probably still gaps in your planning. Nothing reveals those holes and prepares you for your moment in the media spotlight better than conducting several "real-time" crisis drills.

EXERCISE: HOW TO CONDUCT A
"REAL-TIME" CRISIS DRILL

Let's say one of the five possible crises you identified is a major explosion at one of your plants.

1. Begin your crisis drill in the "breaking news" stage. All you know at that point is that an explosion occurred at one of your plants.

    Select a spokesperson and help that person develop messages. Next, conduct an on-camera interview with the selected spokesperson while you and your colleagues play the parts of reporters. Review the video and offer suggestions for improvement.

2. Advance the scenario two hours by moving onto the "reputation-forming" stage. Assume that two workers were killed and at least nine were injured. You still don't know the cause of the accident. Select a spokesperson and repeat the on-camera drill.

3. Advance the scenario to the next day. The media have spoken with several employees who say that management ignored their concerns about the defective equipment that (they claim) caused the accident. You don't know whether that's true, but you're looking into it. Repeat the drill.

Use this exercise as a model to help create relevant real-time scenarios for each of your five crises—and practice, practice, practice! Revise your action plan based on what you learn during your practice interviews.

Reassemble your crisis team at least once per year to review and update your plan.

91 RESPONDING TO BAD PRESS BEFORE THE STORY RUNS

Although this section has dealt exclusively with crisis communications, it's important to note that not all bad press results from a crisis. Sometimes, a reporter gets a key fact wrong, a columnist takes an unfavorable view of your political stance, or an arts critic disapproves of your museum's new exhibit.

Lessons 91 and 92 will help you respond to negative media coverage that doesn't result from a full-fledged crisis but that has the potential to negatively affect your brand. This lesson focuses on how to respond to bad press *before* the story runs.

You can't always respond to stories before publication, since some run without reporters contacting you in advance. But reporters will often ask for your perspective before the story runs, and their questions may make it clear to you that they've drawn incorrect impressions. If you think you're about to be the recipient of bad press, consider these five actions:

1. **Detail the errors:** Make a list of the reporter's errors and explain why the story is wrong. Provide the reporter with the accurate information and cite your sources.

2. **Ask to meet with the reporter:** Little is more disarming than a spokesperson who asks to meet in person. It sends a message that you have nothing to hide and may make reporters reconsider their perspectives.

3. **Take it up a notch:** If you're getting nowhere with the reporter, speak with his or her boss. That person bears greater responsibility for running accurate stories.

4. **Get your lawyers involved:** You may be able to get a story delayed, revised, or killed if you can demonstrate to the news organization that it is factually incorrect and could lead to a costly lawsuit.

5. **Beat the press:** In extreme cases, you might consider releasing your story before the reporter can. That may mean offering the story to a competing (and fairer) journalist or releasing it through your own social media channels. By beating the journalist to the story, you'll be able to get your version of events out first and help control the narrative. But beware: If you pursue this strategy, the reporter may punish you in future coverage.

CAN YOU SUE A NEWS ORGANIZATION FOR AN INCORRECT STORY?

If you're the target of an inaccurate news story, you may be able to sue the offending news organization. The information below comes from Erik M. Pelton & Associates, a law firm specializing in intellectual property and social media issues.

Libel and slander are legal terms for injuring another party by making harmful misstatements. Libel relates to statements made in print or online; slander applies to oral statements. Both are difficult to establish in the U.S., where the person suing has the burden of proof. Claims are easier to prove in many other countries, since the person *accused* of libel or slander has to prove that the disputed statement is true.

In order win a lawsuit in the U.S., the statement must have been negligently made *and* resulted in harm to the person defamed. Public figures have an even higher threshold to meet, and must show the person making the statement knew it to be false or had a reckless disregard for the truth.

To avoid being sued yourself, be sure that any negative statements you make about a specific individual or business are accurate—or are clearly identified as your opinion.

Tread carefully when considering lawsuits against news organizations, since legal cases often attract more headlines and keep damaging information in the headlines that much longer.

92 RESPONDING TO NEGATIVE PRESS AFTER THE STORY RUNS

I'm occasionally asked whether it's ever appropriate to "freeze a reporter out," or refuse to speak to him again.

Whenever I hear that, I immediately think of a scene out of *The Godfather* or *Fatal Attraction*, complete with horse's head and boiled bunny. I imagine frustrated interviewees suddenly appearing as caped crusaders, exacting their revenge on unfair journalists by "rubbing them out."

Think hard before you do that. Freezing a reporter out is a dramatic step that often backfires. After all, you probably think a company is guilty when a newscaster says, "We contacted representatives from the Huge Corporation, but they refused to return our phone calls."

Before blacklisting a reporter, consider these remedies:

1. **Take it to a neutral party:** It's an age-old truth: The closer you are to a news story, the more likely it is you will find it flawed. Ask neutral parties to read, listen to, or watch the story and give you their feedback. You may be surprised to find that the message you hoped would get through to the audience did, indeed, get through.

2. **Talk to the reporter:** Reporters need access to sources to do their jobs, and good reporters are willing to hear their sources' objections to a story (they may not agree with you, but they usually listen). When you speak, remain polite regardless of the response. You will get a better reaction to a discussion about objective factual errors than subjective differences of opinions, but you're welcome to make your case if you believe their view lacks perspective. If they've gotten a key fact wrong, you're entitled to request a correction.

3. **Write a response:** You may have forums available to you for a response, such as a letter to the editor, an op-ed, or a website's comments section. Don't repeat the original errors in your response, since doing so gives those errors more airtime. Just articulate your view.

4. **Speak to the editor:** If you've gotten nowhere with the reporter, you can raise your objections with the reporter's boss. Who knows? You may be the fourth person to complain about the same reporter in the past week. There is a downside here, though—no one likes to be complained about, and the reporter may take it out on you with even less favorable news coverage in the future.

5. **Respond with statements only:** If it's clear that the news organization is irrevocably biased against your company, you have two choices: cut off all access for future stories or respond to subsequent inquiries from that news organization with precision. I usually recommend the latter, which means sending a short written statement in response to future queries. That brief statement prevents the reporter from saying you refused to comment, and gives you more control over the quote.

6. **Cut off all access:** The only time I ever recommend cutting off all access is when there is *nothing* to be gained by speaking to the reporter. Those cases may exist, but they're rare. Most of the time, good media management means finding solutions to working with journalists, not avoiding them altogether.

7. **Use online and social media:** Cutting off access to a news outlet doesn't mean you stop communicating. Use online and social media to continue communicating with your key audiences through all available channels, including your company website and blog, and your corporate social media accounts.

Final Interview Preparation

"Success depends upon previous preparation, and without such preparation there is sure to be failure."

Confucius, Chinese philosopher

93 STEP ONE: COMPLETE YOUR MESSAGE WORKSHEETS

In this section, you will learn seven final steps to take prior to each interview.

The first step is to complete the message worksheets on the following three pages. Complete one for each of your three messages. These messages can be used as overall organizational messages, for an individual campaign, or for a specific topic. The supports beneath each message should reinforce that message.

To help you remember the format, here are the messages and supports about pregnant women in Pennsylvania from earlier in the book:

> *"By loosening Pennsylvania's unreasonable malpractice laws, thousands of pregnant women will be able to find a local obstetrician who can help in case of a medical emergency."*

A story that would fit beneath that message might say:

> *"Jane Jackson, a 26-year-old from Altoona, was in her seventh month of pregnancy last year when she went into labor. She was by herself and called 9-1-1. The paramedics got there in time but didn't have the skills to help when her baby was unable to breathe. Her baby son died. If her skilled obstetrician lived closer, he likely would have been able to save her baby."*

A statistic under that message might say:

> *"More than 18,000 women of childbearing age in Pennsylvania live at least 100 miles from the closest obstetrician."*

A sound bite supporting that message might read:

> *"Having your doctor 100 miles away is kind of like keeping your Band-Aids at a friend's house—they're useless when you need them most."*

MESSAGE 1: _____

_____

_____

STORIES:

1. _____

_____

2. _____

_____

STATISTICS:

1. _____

_____

2. _____

_____

SOUND BITES:

1. _____

_____

2. _____

_____

MESSAGE 2: _____

_____

_____

STORIES:

1. _____

_____

2. _____

_____

STATISTICS:

1. _____

_____

2. _____

_____

SOUND BITES:

1. _____

_____

2. _____

_____

MESSAGE 3: _____

_____

_____

STORIES:

1. _____

_____

2. _____

_____

STATISTICS:

1. _____

_____

2. _____

_____

SOUND BITES:

1. _____

_____

2. _____

_____

94 STEP TWO: CREATE FILE CARDS

Remember that story about my boss who made me rewrite an article three times, telling me to slash it in half each time?

It's my turn to do that to you. I'm not trying to torture you, I promise. But since good communication requires a process of exclusion, I'm going to ask you to distill your information one final time.

That's because most people end up including a lot of details on their message worksheets. That's okay—by filling out your message worksheets, you took a critical step toward excluding everything that wasn't directly related to your top three messages. But if your message worksheets are filled with hundreds of words, you may find them challenging to refer to during a media interview.

The final step is to reduce everything you want to say in the interview—your three messages and your message supports—down to three file cards, one for each message. Here's what your file card may look like for your first message:

LOOSEN LAWS SO WOMEN CAN FIND
   A DOCTOR IN CASE OF EMERGENCY

STORY 1: JANE JACKSON, ALTOONA
STORY 2: DR. PAUL ROBISON, PHILADELPHIA

STAT 1: 18,000 WOMEN LIVE 2100 MILES
         FROM CLOSEST OBSTETRICIAN

STAT 2: 300 OBSTETRICIANS QUIT MEDICINE IN
         PAST 10 YEARS DUE TO LAWS

SOUND BITE 1: "LIKE KEEPING BAND-AIDS AT A
         FRIEND'S HOUSE: USELESS."

SOUND BITE 2: "DON'T OUR WIVES, DAUGHTERS, AND
         CHILDREN DESERVE BETTER?"

Assuming you're familiar enough with the material before your interview—and I hope you are—these file cards should be all you need in front of you during any telephone interview. For television interviews, you shouldn't keep these file cards on your lap, but you can easily refer to them before you go on the air and during any commercial breaks.

File cards have one other advantage: they allow you to sound extemporaneous instead of coming across like you're reading answers off the page. Trimming your message worksheets to just a few phrases allows you to keep the most important points in front of you but prevents you from sounding overly scripted.

You can reduce your file cards even further. Think of the words like golf strokes: the fewer there are, the better your score. You really can deliver a highly focused and effective media interview with nothing in front of you but three file cards like this:

LOOSEN LAWS, WOMEN CAN FIND DOCTOR

- JANE JACKSON
- DR. ROMSON

- 18,000 WOMEN ≥ 100 MILES
- 300 OBSTETRICIAN'S QUIT IN 10 YEARS

- LIKE BAND-AIDS: USELESS
- DON'T WOMEN DESERVE BETTER?

Note: For the sake of this example, I used two stories, two statistics, and two sound bites to reinforce the main message. Feel free to use more message supports—up to three stories, statistics, and sound bites—for each of your three messages.

205

95 STEP THREE: INTERVIEW THE REPORTER

In lesson 2, I mentioned that you shouldn't conduct an interview the moment reporters call. Instead, I advised that you should offer to return their calls promptly, and for you to take at least a few minutes to prepare for the interview before you speak.

But before you hang up from that initial phone call, take a few minutes to "interview" the reporter. Many journalists are willing to share the basics about the stories they're working on, and any insight they offer will help you better prepare.

Below are eight questions you might consider asking reporters. I typically don't ask all of these for every interview, since journalists don't appreciate being grilled. But they'll probably offer some of this information on their own anyway, so just fill in any gaps by asking the most relevant of these questions:

1. **Who are you?** No, you shouldn't ask that question verbatim, but collect the basics—their name, the name of the news organization for which they work, and whether they cover a particular topic.

2. **Can you tell me about the story you're working on?** Keep this question open-ended and remain quiet while the reporter speaks (the more they say, the more you'll learn). Feel free to ask follow-up questions and to clarify any points you don't fully understand.

3. **Are you approaching this story from any particular perspective?** Some reporters will bristle if you ask, "What's your angle?" This question aims to elicit the same information in a more subtle manner.

4. **Who else are you interviewing?** Reporters often play it close to the vest on this one, but it's worth asking. You'll be able to get a sense of the story's tone by learning whether the other

sources in the story are friendly or antagonistic toward your cause.

5. **What's the format?** For print interviews, this question will help you determine whether reporters just need a quick quote from you or whether they're writing an in-depth piece that will focus extensively on your work. For broadcast interviews, you'll be able to learn whether the interview will be live, live-to-tape, or edited. For television, you might also ask if the format will be a remote, on-set, or sound-bites interview.

6. **What do you need from me?** Ask the reporter how much time the interview will last and where the reporter wants to conduct the interview. Also, ask if you can provide any press releases, graphics, photos, videos, or other supplementary documents. You can often expand your presence in a news story—and influence the narrative—if the reporter chooses to use your supporting materials.

7. **Who will be doing the interview?** For many radio and television interviews, you will be contacted initially by an off-air producer rather than by an on-air personality. Ask for the name of the person conducting the interview.

8. **When are you publishing or airing the story?** Review the story as soon as it comes out. If it's a positive story, share it with your online and off-line networks. If it's a negative story, consider issuing a response or contacting the reporter or editor to discuss the coverage.

One final note: Before an interview, tell reporters how you prefer to be identified. Include your title and company name, and spell your full name. Nothing is worse than seeing your name or company's name mangled in front of millions of viewers!

96 STEP FOUR: DO YOUR RESEARCH

After you've spoken (the first time) with the reporter, it's time to put on your sleuth's hat to learn some of the things the journalist *didn't* want to share with you.

It's a simple two-step approach:

1. Research the reporter and the news organization for which he or she works.

2. Research yourself and your company, using the same tools the reporter will likely use.

RESEARCHING THE REPORTER AND THE NEWS ORGANIZATION

First, search for examples of the reporter's work. Many news organizations make their archives available online for little or no cost. It's worth whatever nominal fee the news organization might charge to gain access to a reporter's body of work.

Use search engines such as Google or Yahoo to conduct free research online, and review the reporter's social media pages and those of the news organization for which he or she works.

Read several of the reporter's stories, paying closest attention to those related to your topic, to get a sense of the journalist's tone and approach. You'll quickly get a feel for whether the reporter is a fair arbiter or may employ tactics that will cast your company in a bad light. You'll be able to gauge what misconceptions the reporter has about your topic, which will allow you to spend additional time preparing a rebuttal. And you may also be able to judge whether the reporter is a knowledgeable "beat" reporter who has covered your topic for years or a general-interest reporter who doesn't know much about it.

Take note of whom else the reporter has quoted. If you know any of the people the journalist has spoken with in the past, call them to learn more about their interaction. Also, take note of your opponents who were quoted—knowing who they are and anticipating their criticisms will help you form smart counterarguments.

Finally, learn more about the news organization itself. Is it a primarily neutral news source? Does is it have a liberal or conservative perspective? Is it an edgy and sensationalist outlet?

RESEARCHING YOURSELF AND YOUR COMPANY

Too often, spokespersons forget to turn their sleuthing activities onto themselves, a mistake that blindsides them during their interviews.

At the very least, do a quick online search to see what the reporter will learn about you during his or her research. Search for the following: your name; your name plus your company name; your company name; and your company name plus the names of any associated controversies. Also review your own social media pages and those of your top executives.

Imagine you're a cynical reporter: What might you ask? What questions would you ask about any personal issues, previous scandals, inaccurate past statements, or attacks from opponents? How could you twist your good work into something that looks ill conceived? What holes could you poke in your company's arguments? What controversies about related (or unrelated) topics would you want to know more about?

You can significantly improve your odds of a successful interview by knowing more about the reporter—and what the reporter knows about you.

97 STEP FIVE: DEVELOP A Q&A DOCUMENT

Once you finish interviewing the reporter and conducting your research, you should have a solid understanding of the topics that interest the journalist most. You can use that information to anticipate the questions the reporter is most likely to ask.

Many of our clients like to prepare a question and answer (Q&A) document prior to each interview, in which they list the most likely questions and their responses.

How much time and energy should you devote to such a document? That is a subject of considerable debate among media trainers. Some advocate that you should spend hardly any time trying to anticipate the questions since your goal is simply to return to your messages anyhow. Other trainers regard that advice as hogwash, claiming they regularly anticipate the likeliest questions with ease.

The truth is somewhere in between.

It's a good idea to spend at least some time anticipating the most likely and most challenging questions in advance. As you craft your responses, it's critical to remember that you've already spent a considerable amount of time drafting your top three messages and message supports—so your goal shouldn't be to come up with entirely new answers for each question. Instead, use your message worksheets as a guide to help you craft on-message responses to each of the questions.

Don't try to be comprehensive when creating a Q&A document. If you attempt to list every potential question and rehearse every possible answer, you will likely become paralyzed with too much information—a curse as damaging as too little information. You can strike the perfect balance by following these three steps:

1. Spend 30 minutes brainstorming the most likely questions. Next, spend 30 minutes brainstorming the most potentially damaging questions.

2. Reduce both lists to no more than six questions each.

3. Spend up to one hour developing answers to all 12 questions. That may not seem like a lot of time, but you should be able to answer those questions quickly if you use your message worksheets as a guide.

CASE STUDY: AN OVER-PREPARED EXECUTIVE

One of our clients, a top executive, was preparing for a major launch. Her team had "helpfully" put together a 10-page Q&A document to help her get ready for her upcoming media interviews.

The executive had studied the document thoroughly. But she was trying to remember so much information that she completely froze when we turned the camera on for her practice interview.

To help her focus, I asked her to identify the three most important sentences in the document. Then I asked her to choose one word in each sentence as a memory trigger. When we turned the camera back on, she looked like a different person—confident, well versed, and in control. When she allowed herself to remember less, she uncluttered her mind and become significantly more effective.

To summarize, a Q&A document can be a valuable tool as you prepare for your interview. But keep in mind that the reporter is likely to ask you questions you couldn't or didn't anticipate. Therefore, it's more important to familiarize yourself with your messages and practice the ATMs than it is to brainstorm every possible question and rehearse every possible answer.

98 STEP SIX: CONDUCT A PRACTICE INTERVIEW

There's just one final step before calling reporters back, and that's to record a practice session. Even if the reporter has a particularly bruising deadline, try to do a quick "shortcut" version of this exercise.

This lesson will teach you how to conduct an effective practice session and rate your performance.

RECORD A PRACTICE INTERVIEW

1. Ask colleagues, friends, or family members to interview you. Give them your Q&A document so that they can ask you the questions you developed, but encourage them to ask any relevant follow-up questions they can think of. That will force you to practice answering unanticipated questions by transitioning back to your messages.

2. Supplement your Q&A document with a few open-ended questions (say, "Can you tell me about your company?") and a few of the trap questions you learned earlier in the book.

3. Get your equipment ready. If you're preparing for a television interview, record your practice run with a video camera, if possible. For radio or print interviews, you may use an audio recorder (most smartphones have a built-in audio recording device).

4. Adjust to the format of your upcoming interview. If you're preparing for a standing television "bites" interview, for example, stand up and maintain eye contact with your friend or family member, not the camera. (Your interviewer should stand just to the side of the camera.)

5. When the interview begins, try not to break character. If you make a mistake, keep going. It's important to learn how to

recover from your mistakes, so stay in the moment and do your best to get back to surer ground.

RATE YOUR PERFORMANCE

1. Watch or listen to the tape. Pause the playback after every answer.

2. Begin your self-critique by commenting on the things you did well—positive feedback is important—and then move on to the things you could have done better. Make sure you comment on both the quality of your message and the manner in which you delivered it.

3. After you analyze an answer, ask your colleagues, friends, and/ or family members for their feedback. Proceed through the entire interview, one answer at a time, using this formula.

4. Be kind to yourself. Most people are *much* more critical of themselves than they should be. In media training workshops, people most frequently comment on their age, their looks, or their voice—but the audience is less likely to be distracted by such matters. There's a reason many Academy Award—winning actors refuse to watch their own films—they are painfully self-critical and see only the flaws in their performances. The reality is that their performances were brilliant—and similarly, your performance was likely better than you think.

In the next lesson, you will find 20 specific measurements that will help you identify any trouble spots. Trying to remember 20 things can be paralyzing, so I'll ask you to focus only on the three that will have the greatest impact on your interviewing success.

99 STEP SEVEN: SELECT THREE AREAS FOR IMPROVEMENT

Your head is probably spinning by now. After all, this book describes more than 100 different techniques, and you'll find it impossible to deliver a good media interview if you try to remember all of them the next time you speak to a reporter.

THIS LESSON WILL HELP YOU REDUCE EVERYTHING YOU'VE LEARNED TO JUST THREE THINGS YOU NEED TO REMEMBER.

Review the checklist below. Circle the three items you need to improve upon most. During your next interview, focus primarily on those three points. If you improve in *just those three areas,* you're virtually guaranteed a better media performance. Once you improve upon those areas, add a fourth item. When you improve upon that one, add a fifth, and so on.

YOUR MESSAGE

1. Each of my answers contains at least one message or message support.

2. My messages are aligned with the audience's needs.

3. Many of my answers include a story, statistic, or sound bite.

4. I answer off-topic or difficult questions using the ATMs.

5. I recognize trap questions and avoid taking the bait.

6. I answer challenging questions with a welcoming tone and without defensiveness.

7. I deliver my answers in 30 seconds or less, and pause for a few seconds before answering questions (for edited interviews).

8. I use jargon-free, strong, everyday language.

9. I remember to speak to my "target person."

10. I begin my answers with the headline.

11. I answer open-ended "what" questions with the "why + what."

YOUR VOICE AND BODY LANGUAGE

12. I vary my vocal delivery (pitch, pace, volume) to help emphasize key points.

13. I come across as warm, likeable, and "real."

14. I sound and/or look confident.

15. My energy level conveys an appropriate sense of excitement about my topic.

16. I maintain strong eye contact.

17. I use natural gestures and don't appear "stiff."

18. I use proper posture and avoid positions that make me appear passive, arrogant, or uninterested.

19. I avoid unnecessary distractions, such as using verbal filler, shuffling in my chair, or blinking repeatedly.

20. My attire, makeup, and hair is "television-friendly."

In addition to using this list to help you prepare for interviews, you can use it to help evaluate your performance *after* each interview. Following each interview, critique yourself using the 20 measurements above, and take notes about the areas in which you want to continue improving. Remember to review your notes prior to your next interview.

Conclusion

"*If it's called the* USA Today, *why is all the news from yesterday? BAM. Busted!*"

Stephen Colbert, Comedian

100 HOW TO SELECT A MEDIA TRAINER

I hope this book helps you grow dramatically as a media spokesperson. But no book can fully take the place of experiencing an on-camera media training session with an experienced trainer who fires unexpected questions at you.

If you need media training, I hope you'll select my firm, Phillips Media Relations. But I would do you a disservice if I suggested mine is the only qualified firm; there are many terrific media trainers out there (and more than a few duds). Here are 11 questions you should ask when shopping for a media trainer:

1. **Does the firm "look" professional?** If the company doesn't have a professional-looking website, it's probably a sign that you're looking at someone who dabbles in media training instead of someone making a career of it.

2. **Does the firm have high-quality references?** The best marketing is a happy client. Call or email three of the firm's clients. If the company is unwilling or unable to provide three quality references, move on.

3. **Who will be doing the training?** Larger companies don't always send the firm's principal to do your training. Find out who would do the training, how often they train, and get references for the trainer and the firm.

4. **What is the tone of the workshop?** Good trainers are high on the EQ (emotional intelligence) scale—that is, they are able to sense the vulnerabilities of their trainees and adjust their styles to match the needs of the group.

5. **Is the workshop customized?** Media training should be completely customized. For a full-day workshop, we develop numerous questions specific to the company and use examples

218

from the client's industry. If the firm uses a canned "off-the-shelf" presentation, run the other way.

6. **Does the trainer have journalism experience?** Journalism experience is critical in a good media trainer. Someone who has only worked in public relations has never experienced firsthand the pressures reporters face.

7. **Does the trainer have training experience?** Many former journalists call themselves media trainers, but few begin as experienced workshop facilitators. Journalism experience is one thing—but if trainers don't have extensive experience as instructors, forget it.

8. **Does the trainer have industry experience?** I've never believed this should be a deal breaker. Too much industry knowledge can prevent a trainer from seeing the 35,000-foot level, meaning both trainer and trainee spend too much time in the weeds. Trainers should be expert in the *process* of helping spokespersons refine their messages and deliver them well—not necessarily in the *content*.

9. **Does the firm offer post-training education?** No one can learn everything in a single day of training. What does the firm do to extend the education past the training day? Does it offer follow-up phone calls, newsletters, blog articles, videos, and/or other learning opportunities?

10. **Does the firm have a blog, a book, or published articles?** Read everything you can by the firm. Read its blog, published articles, and/or its book. Make sure you're comfortable with the approach to training.

11. **What is the firm's standing in the industry?** Is it a lone wolf or an industry thought leader? Is it a regularly quoted expert source?

101 GO OUT THERE AND GET 'EM!

If you're like most of our clients, you won't have media interviews scheduled on a daily basis. For most spokespersons, media interviews occur somewhat sporadically, sometimes weeks or months apart.

But if you don't practice your new media skills, they'll atrophy before you ever have a chance to use them.

What now?

First, one of the great things about media training—any type of communications training, really—is that you can practice many of these skills in your day-to-day life.

As examples:

- When the person seated beside you on the plane asks what you do, try out your "why + what."

- When you spend time with your young cousins, tell them what you do for a living while remembering the 12-year-old-nephew rule.

- When a colleague asks your opinion about a sensitive work decision, pause for a few seconds so you can deliver a more fully formed answer.

- Next time you argue with your spouse, remember to avoid any "seven-second strays" (or you'll be reminded of your momentary gaffe for the next week—or longer!).

Second, do every interview you possibly can. If you work for a company, volunteer to be the spokesperson for every small, seemingly inconsequential media interview it can arrange.

Internet radio show with 200 listeners? Excellent. A small website that looks like it gets 20 visitors per week? Perfect.

Adopt the attitude that there's no news organization "too small" to invest time in, and you'll get many more opportunities to practice your skills. Plus, if you blow the interview (it happens), odds are you won't do a lot of damage.

Finally, please stay involved with our community to keep building your skills and interacting with other budding media spokespersons. You can begin by visiting our blog at www.MrMediaTraining.com.

We update the blog several times each week with tips for media spokespersons and public speakers. You'll also find our take on the hottest news stories of the moment from a communications perspective. Plus, we regularly post videos of spokespersons doing it right—and failing spectacularly. I hope you'll become a regular visitor.

You can sign up for our email newsletter directly from the blog. I also interact with readers through social media. You can follow me on Twitter at www.twitter.com/MrMediaTraining or like me on Facebook at www.facebook.com/MrMediaTraining.

Please drop me an email to let me know how you're doing along the way. You can find me at Brad@PhillipsMediaRelations.com.

I'm delighted that you chose to invest in making yourself a more effective spokesperson and am thrilled that you chose me as your media trainer. Thank you.

Acknowledgments

First, I owe an enormous debt of gratitude to my firm's clients. You've allowed me to gain an insider's view into your media challenges and concerns, and I can only hope that you've learned as much from me as I have from you.

I'm equally grateful to the readers of the Mr. Media Training Blog. You have not only given me the opportunity to try out some of these lessons on the blog before refining them for this book, but you've challenged me in several places to reconsider my conclusions. The insightful comments and questions you regularly leave on the blog provided a lot of the fodder for the book. I am humbled by your loyal readership.

To the bloggers and editors who have supported me through the years, thank you for helping the world discover my work. Taegan Goddard of Political Wire, David Mark of Politix (and formerly *Politico*), and Michael Sebastian of PR Daily have been especially generous, but there are many others. You know who you are, and I thank you.

Dave Groobert, Tod Ibrahim, and Christina Mozaffari (our firm's senior media trainer) not only reviewed my manuscript but also offered in-depth and perceptive feedback. This book is markedly better as a result of your thoughtful suggestions.

Wayne Bloom, Linda Carlisle, Richard Harris, Russ Mittermeier, Jack Hayes, Susan Buchanan, Joan Stewart, Jeff Domansky, and Jane Jordan-Meier took time out of their busy schedules to review the book and offer testimonials. I was amazed that so many busy executives made time for this project. I don't take your commitment for granted.

Ari Ashe of WTOP-FM and Bob Andelman of Mr. Media Interviews (unrelated to my similarly named blog) both lent their deep expertise to this book's radio lessons.

Luba Vangelova helped write the five makeup lessons in this book, and Lillian Brown, Deborah Boland and JoJami Tyler of TV Image Live, Rebecca Perkins, and Ingrid Grimes-Miles contributed their expertise related to clothing, makeup, and hair.

Erik Pelton, my friend and attorney, never seemed to tire of my endless legal questions.

I'm fortunate to have worked with a terrific editor. Andrew Rosenberg lent his tremendous talents to this project, and this book is far better as a result. Plus, he was a joy to work with.

To my mother, who revels in my every success, and my father, from whom I inherited my entrepreneurial drive.

Finally, to my wife, Jessica, who suffered far too many lonely nights (and a distracted husband) as I labored on this book. I couldn't have done this without the positive energy and inspiration you give me. I love you, babe.

Sources

Lesson 10: Plouffe, David. *The Audacity to Win: The Inside Story of Barack Obama's Historic Victory.* New York: Viking Adult, 2009.

Lessons 11 & 18: Heath, Chip, and Dan Heath. *Made to Stick: Why Some Ideas Survive and Others Die.* New York: Random House, 2007.

Lessons 12 & 17: Luntz, Frank I. *Words That Work: It's Not What You Say, It's What People Hear.* New York: Hyperion, 2006.

Lesson 21: Yudkin, Marcia. *The Sound Bite Workbook: How to Generate Snappy Tag Lines, Scintillating Interview Quotes, Captivating Book or Article Titles, and Irresistible Marketing or Publicity Handles.* Goshen, MA: Creative Ways Publishing, 2011.

Lesson 48: Gladwell, Malcolm. *Blink: The Power of Thinking Without Thinking. New York:* Back Bay Books, 2007.

Lessons 50 & 51: Pease, Allan, and Barbara Pease. *The Definitive Book of Body Language.* New York: Bantam, 2006.

Lessons 56—59: Brown, Lillian. *Your Public Best: The Complete Guide to Making Successful Public Appearances, Second Edition.* New York: William Morrow, 2002.

Lesson 61: Thornton, Robert J. *The Lexicon of Intentionally Ambiguous Recommendations (L.I.A.R.).* Naperville, IL: Sourcebooks Hysteria, 2003.

Lesson 66: Stahl, Lesley. *Reporting Live.* New York: Simon & Schuster, 1999.

Lesson 79: Knight, Rory F, and Deborah J. Pretty (1996). "The Impact of Catastrophes on Shareholder Value." Research report, Oxford, UK, 1996.

Lessons 79, 83 & 86: Jordan-Meier, Jane. *The Four Stages of Highly Effective Crisis Management: How to Manage the Media in the Digital Age.* Boca Raton, FL: CRC Press, 2011.

Lessons 83 & 89: Dezenhall, Eric, and John Weber. *Damage Control: The Essential Lessons of Crisis Management.* Westport, CT: Prospecta Press, 2011.

Photo Credits

All photos are used with permission from iStockPhoto (www.iStockPhoto.com), unless noted otherwise below:

Hubert Humphrey: Public domain, photographer unknown

Mark McGwire: Screen grab from C-SPAN television; full video at: http://www.c-spanvideo.org/program/185904-2

Carly Fiorina: Screen grab from CNN; full video at http://politicalticker.blogs.cnn.com/2010/06/09/open-mic-catches-fiorina-dig-at-boxer/?fbid=D9zkm9BH5Pk

Mark Twain: Public domain; photographers unknown

Hierarchy of Needs: Wikimedia Commons; image credit: Factoryjoe

Sam Donaldson: Photo credit: ABC News

Russ Mittermeier: CI / Russell A. Mittermeier

Richard Nixon: Associated Press, used with permission

Tammy Faye Bakker: From Wikimedia Commons; photo credit: Darwin Bell

Laura Bush: Public domain; photo credit: Krisanna Johnson

Don King: Wikimedia Commons; photo credit: Shawn Lea

Sally Jesse Raphael: Wikimedia Commons; photo credit: David Shankbone

Marshall McLuhan: Public domain; photographer unknown

President John F. Kennedy: Public domain; photo credit: Cecil Stoughton

About Phillips Media Relations

Phillips Media Relations (PMR) is one of the nation's premier media training, presentation training, and crisis communications training firms.

Since our founding in 2004, we have trained thousands of spokespersons for interviews seen by more than 1 billion people worldwide.

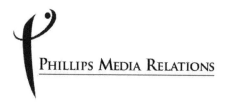

We're broadly experienced with a wide variety of clients. We've helped thousands of corporate executives, nonprofit leaders, government officials, scientists, and many others prepare for media interviews and public presentations.

We've earned a reputation as one of the industry's primary thought leaders, and are regularly cited as experts by major news organizations, influential public relations journals, and popular news websites.

Our clients are regularly surprised by the extensive amount of research we conduct prior to each training. They often tell us that our training was not only the most effective they've ever had but also significantly more enjoyable than they expected.

We have offices in New York City and Washington, DC.

To learn more about our firm and find out how we can help you, please visit www.PhillipsMediaRelations.com or email us at Info@ PhillipsMediaRelations.com.

About The Mr. Media Training Blog

The Mr. Media Training Blog offers daily tips to help readers become better media spokespersons and public speakers.

Our active community of readers visits each day to learn new tips they can implement into their media interviews immediately, to see how public figures are faring in their communications, and to watch videos of media successes (and media disasters).

On any given day, you might find articles such as:

- Five Things to Remember Before Your Next Television Appearance

- Seven Rules to Remember in a Crisis

- Twelve Things 1980s Music Teaches You About Public Speaking

- The Ten Worst Media Disasters of the Year

- How to Survive an Ambush Interview

Mr. Media Training (www.MrMediaTraining.com) is the world's most visited media training website*, with tens of thousands of visitors each month.

(*Source: Alexa, December 2012)

About Brad Phillips

Brad Phillips is the president of Phillips Media Relations, a media, presentation, and crisis communications training firm with offices in New York City and Washington, DC.

Mr. Phillips has trained thousands of media spokespersons, is regularly quoted as an expert by the media, and writes the world's most-visited media training website, the Mr. Media Training Blog.

One of the best-known media trainers in the United States, Mr. Phillips has also trained clients in Central and South America, Europe, and Asia.

He has worked with hundreds of top-level executives, including corporate CEOs, presidents of nonprofit organizations and trade associations, and directors of government agencies.

He is a sought-after media expert, having been quoted by *USA Today*, *The Washington Post*, Fox News Channel, WTOP Radio, the Associated Press, *The Miami Herald*, *The New York Observer*, *Chicago Tribune*, the Huffington Post, *The Hill*, and many other news outlets.

He is a weekly contributor to *Politico's* "The Arena" and a frequent contributor to Ragan's PR Daily, one of the world's most popular public relations websites.

Mr. Phillips founded Phillips Media Relations in 2004 after working for several years as a broadcast journalist. After beginning his career as an on-air radio announcer, Mr. Phillips worked for *ABC's Nightline with Ted Koppel*, where he contributed to broadcasts about everything from the declining national savings rate and school shootings to domestic politics and terrorism.

He then moved to CNN, where he helped produce two weekly programs: the media analysis program, *Reliable Sources*, and the political roundtable, *The Capital Gang*. He was also a contributing producer to the Sunday public affairs program, *Late Edition with Wolf Blitzer*.

Mr. Phillips has served as a broadcast journalism judge for the prestigious Robert F. Kennedy Journalism Awards, which recognize news programs for outstanding reporting of problems of the disadvantaged.

Quantity Discounts

We offer a quantity discount on the paperback edition of *The Media Training Bible* for groups interested in purchasing 20 copies or more.

If you represent a corporation, nonprofit organization, government agency, academic institution, or group, and would like to inquire about receiving a quantity discount, please email us at Books@ SpeakGoodPress.com.

Made in the USA
San Bernardino, CA
22 July 2019